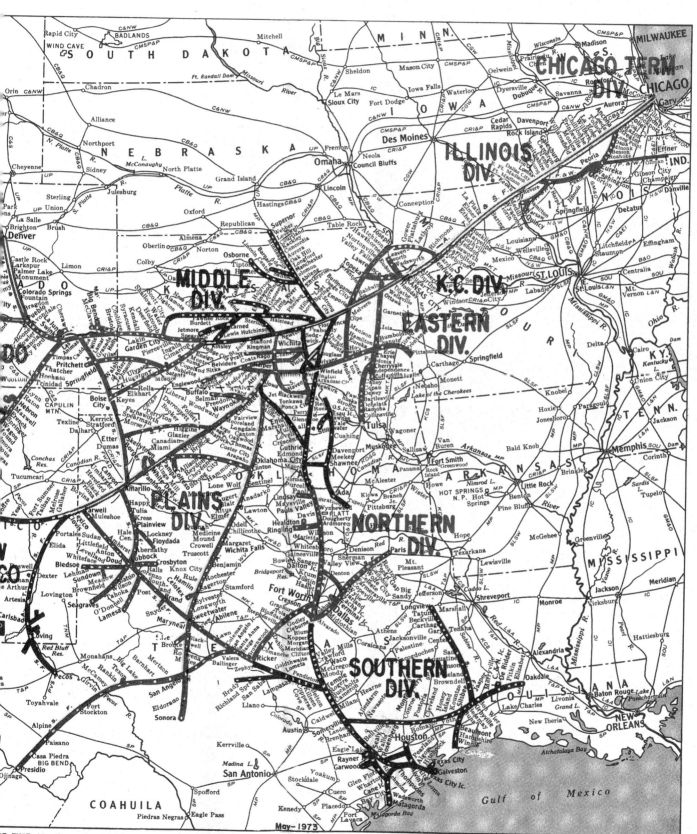

May- 1973

MILEAGE OPERATED
Atchison, Topeka and Santa Fe Ry......**12,557.11** miles

Santa Fe Passenger Trains in the Streamlined Era

By Patrick C. Dorin

Travel on the Santa Fe - All the Way

2004
TLC Publishing, Inc.
18292 Forest Rd.
Forest, VA 24551

TABLE OF CONTENTS

International Standard Book Number: 1-883089-99-9
Library of Congress Catalog Card Number: 2004110163
Design & Layout by
Megan Johnson
Johnson 2 Studios, Rustburg, Va.

Printed in USA
by Walsworth Publishing Co., Marceline, Mo.

Title Page Caption: This photo shows another chapter in the Super Chief History with 4 F units with a total of 6000 horsepower and the Pleasure Dome Lounge Car 6 cars back in the consist. The All-Pullman train is running through the National Forest just west of Flagstaff, Arizona. (Santa Fe Railway, Harry Stegmaier Collection)

ACKNOWLEDGMENTS

The author wishes to thank all of the people for their kind assistance with the writing of the Santa Fe book, for without their wisdom, knowledge, library of photographs, timetables, passenger train ads, and a host of other materials; the book would never had been completed.

My wife, Karen, continues to be supportive with insights and encouragement for my writing. Without her wisdom and ideas to begin with, none of the books would ever have even gotten started.

Tom Dixon of TLC Publishing has been a tremendous inspiration for this book and many others. Megan Johnson worked with the layout and editing for the book. Patricia Michaelis, Sara Keckeisen, Debbie Greeson, Lin Fredericksen, Lisa Keys and Barry Worley from the Kansas State Historical Society assisted with file and photo searches including the photo reproductions. Much of the Santa Fe Railway materials are now housed at the Kansas State Historical Society in Topeka, Kansas. Coi Gehrig of the Denver Public Library provided assistance and reproduction of photos from the Otto Perry Collection.

Patrick Hiatte, Fred Rutt, and Teena Wester of the BNSF provided information and sources for photos of both ATSF & BNSFequipment. Sermeng Tay-Konkol and Dennis Pehoski of Wm. K. Walthers, Inc. assisted with information and photos on modeling Santa Fe passenger equipment.

Many other photos, timetables and materials were provided by many people including Thomas Dorin, Michael Dorin, Harold K. Vollrath, J. Michael Gruber, David R. Carlson, Russ Isbrandt, Dan Mackey, Bill Jelinek, Harry Stegmaier, and Herman Page. Clifford Prather, Al Chione, Jeff Koeller, William S. Kuba, John Sward, Bob's Photos, Bob Bullerman, Joe Stark, and Marvin Nielsen.

Gilford Spencer and Kevin Peterson of the Duluth Camera Exchange assisted with the reproduction of many photographs. Ellen Kotera and Hart Ziegler of Tri-State Business Systems (Superior) assisted with a wide variety of work including copying and arranging materials for their ultimate use in the book.

Without the kind assistance and time from these folks, the book would never have been assembled. I cannot emphasize enough the importance of this for the creation of our railroad books.

If any name has been inadvertently left out of the above lists, we trust it will be in the appropriate area within the text.

DEDICATION

Dedicated To
John Sward
Longtime Friend, Railroad Researcher
And Did
Service Design and Marketing Research
For The
Santa Fe Railway

INTRODUCTION

A horn is heard as a head light gleams in the distance. The sound and light are at least a mile away but within 36 seconds, the passenger train with an incredible red and silver color scheme are blowing the for the adjacent grade crossing. The silver train, which originated at Chicago's Dearborn Station, streaks by at 100 miles per hour as it heads for its Los Angeles destination. The observation car is already fading off into the distance as this remarkable example of a SANTA FE CHIEF continues its westward journey.

Yes, indeed, the Santa Fe was a remarkable rail passenger carrier for decades, and especially from the late 1930s through to the Amtrak Date of May 1, 1971. The equipment was spotless inside and out, the crews were a delight to talk with, and just simply riding a Santa Fe passenger train brought about a sense of peace and tranquility. It was truly the "Way to Go - The Santa Fe All the Way."

The purpose of this book is to survey the Santa Fe passenger train services, which included through and fast streamliner and domeliners, exceptionally important secondary main line passenger trains, mail and express services, branch and local operations, and some very interesting "Corridor Services" in California - known as the Golden Gates and the San Diegans. In fact, the only passenger service the company did not offer were commuter train services. Ironically, however, there were people who did ride the Santa Fe from Joliet to Chicago for shopping and other activities. The Chicago - Joliet segment did have commuter train services from both the Rock Island and the Gulf, Mobile and Ohio.

Amtrak has been in operation for over 32 years as of this writing during the fall of 2003. Superliner trains operate between Chicago and Los Angeles, which in some ways, resemble the "Hi-level" cars built for the El Capitan. Furthermore, Amtrak operates the fleet of trains once known as the San Diegans between LA and San Diego. The fleet is presently known as the Surfliners. And if that is not enough, commuter train services are now operated on segments and former segments of the Santa Fe in the LA - San Diego area. Known as MetroLink and the Coaster in the LA and San Diego areas respectively.

It is interesting to note that as we move deeper into the 21st Century, there are more passenger trains operating between LA and San Diego than ever. Just one part of the Coaster and Amtrak train services means 44 passenger trains a day for San Diego. It just goes to show it is only RAILROAD SYSTEMS that can alleviate traffic congestion and improve safety for travel of all types - but that is another story.

To get back on the Santa Fe track, the book covers the various types of train services as well as equipment and passenger motive power. It is hoped that the information provided will give insights into future passenger services, generate pleasant memories about one incredible railroad (which truly had a sense of community both within the company and with its passengers and shippers), and will add to the information needed for the Art of Model Railroading, especially Santa Fe passenger services. Fortunately, one can still travel on the Santa Fe trackage between Chicago and Los Angeles as well as the route to San Diego.

SHIP AND TRAVEL THE SANTA FE - ALL THE WAY

Patrick C. Dorin
July 1, 2004
Superior, Wisconsin

Passenger Train Consists are part of the various chapters with a variety of symbols as follows:

Combn	Combination Car
LCD	Lunch Counter Dining Car
CC	Chair Car
BE	Baggage Express
SM	Storage Mail
EM	Express and Mail
BEM	Baggage, Express and Mail
BM	Baggage and Mail
DH	Dead Head – Meaning the move ment of an empty car for a new Assignment
RPO	Railway Post Office
COF	Containers on Flat Cars
P. Box	Box cars equipped with steamlines and high speed trucks for Storage mail or express service

Chapter 1 - SANTA FE ALL THE WAY

The Santa Fe Railway offered one of the most comprehensive passenger services to be found on any railroad. What is even more important is the positive attitude that the company had with and for passengers as well as for freight shippers. One of the biggest goals on a day to day basis was to provide reliable, clean and on time services to fit the needs of the traveling public. There is much to learn from the Santa Fe regarding their policy for reliable service that could and should be applied to not only railroad but all transportation services in North America.

The Santa Fe was constantly monitoring customer needs, and made changes based on those needs. The philosophy was literally in effect until the very end of the Santa Fe services, and actually beyond. The company originally did not want to join Amtrak and had wanted to adjust the passenger services to meet cost elements and still provide a decent transcontinental service. However, Santa Fe did become part of the Amtrak system in 1971 with but one passenger train in operation between Chicago and Los Angeles. What were some of the many things that the Santa Fe did to win passengers, actually make a profit, and continue its positive image with the traveling and shipping public? Let's look at a series of such activities from 1946 until 1969 and there were many of them.

A quick look back to the turn of the century, the Santa Fe was operating top class passenger trains, which set the base line for operations over the next 70 years. Just one example was the *California Limited*. The train was established around 1892 and it operated over the 2,265 mile route from Chicago to Los Angeles in 83 hours westbound, and 82 hours eastbound. The usual consist of the train in those days was 10 cars, which included a chair car, tourist sleeping cars, "Palace" sleeping cars and a dining car. The All-Pullman *Super Chief* made the run in under 40 hours in 1950. Things just kept rolling along.

The Santa Fe, as with many other railroads, began looking for ways to improve passenger services right after World War II. During that hectic and serious period of time, the railroad had literally no time to think. The big job was to keep the trains running and handling thousands upon thousands of military personnel.

The company began a series of new plans and train operations which covered the various *Chiefs*, plus new ones, and the *El Capitan* as well as the many other train services offered by the company. One of the first in 1946, but not the first new service, was the offering of transcontinental Pullman sleeping car service between New York and Los Angeles. The all room car departed New York City on the New York Central's *Twentieth Century*, and was transferred to the Santa Fe's *Chief* in Chicago. This meant that the car had to be transferred from the La Salle Street Station in Chicago to the Dearborn Station. Passengers could either stay onboard the car during the transfer, or they could get off and enjoy Chicago for a bit and go over to the other station. Eastbound, Santa Fe handled the car in the *Chief* and was transferred to the NYC's *Twentieth Century Limited* in Chicago. In effect, the transcontinental run offered third morning arrival at both destinations. It was a nice way to enjoy some time away from the hectic world, relax and watch the country roll by.

This type of innovation was the result of several meetings the company held in 1946. The meetings covered the new information regarding train services, equipment, the variety of new schedules. These were described in detail with discussions with the passenger department representatives from all over the U.S. The information also included data of ticket rates and tariffs, dining and lounge car services, how to work with prospective passengers, courtesy, baggage handling and many other areas pertinent to passenger services.

The meetings were not meant to be purely educational in nature with a series of orders of how to do what and when. The meetings were also held so that people could renew acquaintances and friendships. The company understood the importance of a sense of community for working with and for the staff, as well as working with and for passengers and shippers. The positive attitude about people was most important in the eyes of the corporate Santa Fe.

Fred Gurley, the president of the Santa Fe, stressed

The Santa Fe set up advertising in their time tables, such as the opportunity to secure Santa Fe Movies from the company Film Bureau

this concept in a series of meetings and in an article in RAILWAY AGE, November 15, 1947. He pointed out the various things the Santa Fe was doing to meet the challenge, and how the company was working to improve the comfort levels and economy of rail passenger travel. He pointed out the success of the new *Super Chief* and *El Capitan* as just two examples of what can be done to work with passengers.

Mr. Gurley also pointed out in 1948 more things about the success of the railroad's approach to the passenger traffic. The Santa Fe passenger revenues had increased 220 percent in 1947 since the *Super Chief* had been placed in operation in 1936. In fact, when the *Super Chief* was placed in operation, the passenger revenues were only 40 percent of what they had been at the start of the Great Depression in 1929. He pointed out that by adding trains, such as the increased frequencies of the *Super Chief* and *El Capitan*, they were able to expand with equipment and services equal to the demands of the post-war passenger travel. Mr. Gurley stressed the importance of meeting the needs of the public if a passenger service were to be successful. (RAILWAY AGE, March 6, 1948)

The Santa Fe came up with a new passenger time table for transcontinental passengers in 1948. This timetable contained scenic information, such as tunnels and rivers. The eastbound and westbound schedules of the transcontinental trains were shown separately on opposite pages. This made it easier for passengers to read.

The timetables were placed in all accommodations for use by the passengers. Other information included the time of river crossings and other scenic areas, mileages, and altitudes. Train connections were also part of each time table making it easier for passengers to determine their connecting trains.

The Santa Fe and the New York Central looked at the idea of a Coast-to-Coast train in 1950, but that never materialized. On the other hand, the Santa Fe kept up its zest for a positive image for passenger services with the establishment of new ticket offices. Two examples were created in 1951 and 1952.

The new passenger office in Fort Worth, Texas was completed first. It had a simple functional design with a touch of Navajo styling. A serpentine ticket counter with a drop light panel above added a note of informality contrasting with the straight lines of the brick walls and the glass front. Plant boxes at the front window replaced the usual store-window type display cases. There were several comfortable chairs with side tables for magazines while prospective passengers waited to be served.

The next new one in 1952 was placed at Beverly Hills, California. Passengers requesting tickets, information and itineraries dealt with the ticket clerks while seated at a desk height counter. A curved leather covered settee below an oil painting provided additional seating for prospective - and better yet - repeat passengers.

Early in 1952, an advertising summary was mailed out to all travel and ticket agents. The Santa Fe emphasized its full-color travel promotion ads scheduled for printing in a large number of popular magazines. The contents of the material mailed indicated how the new set of ads were sup-

Another example of an ad was the Indian Museum in Albuquerque. (Jan. 1954, page 35.)

ported by displays and posters for travel bureaus, department stories and luggage stores. It also included travel folders and a library of travel motion pictures. Travel agents were encouraged to use the materials freely. It was still another way that the Santa Fe was working to get the message across about the convenience of rail travel.

Still another area of importance for passenger travel is clean passenger equipment, both inside and out. The railroad meticulously took care of this concept not only at the main terminals, such as Chicago, Los Angeles and elsewhere; but also at intermediate stations. For example, the company placed in service movable washers at Albuquerque, New Mexico to handle exterior car washing on six trains each way daily. The fast, economical method of cleaning the exteriors and car windows literally added to the passenger's enjoyment.

Speaking of promotion and advertising, the Santa Fe entered into a cooperative working relationship with Macy's Department Store in Kansas City in 1953. A group of "Travel by Train" windows featured different aspects of train travel. It showed such concepts as riding in a dome car, and the comfort of Pullman sleeping cars. Each of the windows created represented a different car in a passenger train.

The Santa Fe came up with a new reservation system in 1956, which eliminated a great deal of waiting time, and avoided different types of errors. A passenger could make a reservation, and have the information and confirmation almost immediately. It was one of the first computer systems used for such operations. Furthermore, the reservation system could handle interline movements or travel between the Santa Fe and the eastern railroads. This enhanced ticket sales more effectively with positive results for one and all. Offices were equipped relatively quickly with the system. Chicago, of course, being one of the first at the railroad's Chicago Travel Center.

Moving into the late 1950s, the Santa Fe's positive approach for passenger traffic continued. The company had launched a program known as "Good Service" as well

Condensed Schedules Transcontinental Trains

WEST— Read down — Rules for Trains No. 17, 18, 19, 20, 21 and 22 Shown on Page 61.

For explanation of Reference Marks see pages 8 and 9.

EAST— Read up

(Condensed transcontinental train schedule table from the January, 1947 Time Table, listing Train Nos. 3, 1, 21, 17, 19, 23, Stations (Central Standard Time, Mountain Standard Time, Pacific Standard Time), and Train Nos. 24, 20, 4, 18, 22, 2, with principal stations including Chicago, Joliet, Streator, Chillicothe, Galesburg Ill., Ft. Madison La., Shopton, Marceline, Henrietta, Kansas City, Lawrence Kan., Topeka, Emporia, Strong City, Florence, Newton, Hutchinson, Dodge City, Garden City, Syracuse Kan., La Junta Colo., Pueblo, Colorado Springs, Denver, Trinidad Colo., Raton N.M., Las Vegas, Lamy, Albuquerque, Newton, Wichita, Wellington Kan., Canadian Tex., Pampa, Amarillo Tex., Clovis N.M., Clovis, Vaughn, Belen, Gallup N.M., Holbrook Ariz., Winslow, Flagstaff, Williams, Grand Canyon, Ash Fork, Prescott, Phoenix, Seligman Ariz., Needles Cal., Barstow, San Bernardino, Pasadena, Long Beach, Los Angeles, San Diego, Barstow, Bakersfield, Fresno, Merced, Stockton, Berkeley, Oakland, San Francisco.)

Time shown in light figures indicates a.m. Time shown in dark figures indicates p.m.

The Santa Fe operated a vast fleet of transcontinental passenger trains, such as illustrated with the Condensed Schedules from the January, 1947 Time Table.

And incidently, the *El Capitan* was an Extra Fare train to California. It is interesting to note, that the cash sales of *El Capitan* tickets in Chicago increased by 56% from 1956 to 1957. However, if the Santa Fe had not provided reliable and comfortable services levels, there would not have been any increases. In fact, the downward spiral would have simply continued without faltering.

The Santa Fe continued to look for ways to meet passenger and shipper needs. In 1958, the company improved the transportation into San Francisco with a bus connection from Richmond. This saved time (15 minutes or more) for passengers as well as money for the company. Previously, the train to bus transfer took place at Oakland. Thus, the company eliminated the deadhead train movements between the Richmond terminal and Oakland. The Santa Fe Motor Coach subsidiary purchased new buses with a seating capacity for 41 passengers for the service.

All of the railroads during the 1950s experienced passenger deficits. However, the Santa Fe deficit was lower in 1958 compared to 1957. Part of the success had to do with the promotion and reliability of the main line passenger service.

as continued passenger-sales meetings throughout the Santa Fe system. Agents and sales representatives promoted both passenger and freight services. What is most interesting about this is that it widened the Santa Fe's reputation. And it brought in many positive results. For example, the 1956 revenues were 6.8% higher than 1955. Neighboring railroads, meanwhile, continued to face declining markets.

One has to remember, however, that the sales techniques alone did not promote the Santa Fe passenger growth. The *El Capitan* continued to see increases in patronage. In fact, the *El Capitan's* summer passenger traffic in 1957 was 12% above that of 1956.

The superb passenger equipment, which provided high comfort levels, accounted for part of the continued increase. By this time, the Santa Fe's *El Capitan* was equipped with the new "Hi-Level" equipment. (See chapter 2) The company extensively advertised the *El Capitan's* features as well as the all important "Lower-than-Air" fares.

Branch line services with little or no patronage at all were discontinued. (See Chapter 4, Local and Branch Line Passenger Services)

It is most interesting to note that the Santa Fe's passenger revenues had increased every year for five years from 1956 through 1961. Again, it had to do with positive promotional systems, maintaining high quality services, and a willingness to look at new ideas to serve the traveling public. One component was the "Tom-Tom" Program. This was a travel tip program for all Santa Fe employees and their families. Santa Fe people were encourage to provide tips for the marketing departments. About 50% of the leads resulted in ticket sales, which brought in total revenues of $125,000 in 1961. (RAILWAY AGE, May 21, 1962)

It was the belief that every Santa Fe person is a potential traffic salesman. There is more to this than meets the eye, and it is something that should be practiced by all organizations. An entire book could be written on this concept of working relationships.

However, because the Santa Fe had this overall philosophy, it added to the strength and reputation of the railroad. Various types of prizes were given to employees who came up with the tips.

Another positive element was the "Dining Club". This was a meal book for five meals with a price of $10.00. This permitted passengers to budget the cost of meals for trips, and to obtain a full course meal at lower than the regular prices. This proved to be successful and was expanded for several trains.

The Santa Fe also launched a "Go Now - Pay Later" plan. This too brought in additional passengers that otherwise would not have traveled, let along rode the Santa Fe.

The railroad also began an experimentation with a one-third fare reduction between Los Angeles and San Diego to enhance the competition with highway and air transportation. (By the way, as a Side Note: If Amtrak were not running the Surf Lines on the LA - San Diego route, there would be substantial increases in air traffic and highway traffic congestion. Again, it shows only rail can solve the congestion problems.)

The Santa Fe also launched a baggage cart program for passengers. It first stated the program in 1954 at Topeka, Kansas. Passengers really appreciated it, and the company eventually expanded the program at 35 stations. The service was noted in the time tables.

Santa Fe passenger revenues continued to grow in the early 1960s. The 1962 revenues of over $41.8 million were 2.1% higher than in 1961's $40.9 million. The Santa Fe attributed the growth to the family fare plans, dining club books, and the Go Now - Pay Later Plan. However, what was even more important was the working with the crews and staff. A series of meetings were continually held throughout the system. The meetings were designed for open discussions about the passenger traffic performance, passenger complaints, and suggestions for improvements and meeting passenger and traffic needs. The meetings were attended by train crews, car attendants, dining car personnel, agents, mechanical department staffs, and a wide number of representatives from many employee groups. This created a positive atmosphere, which in turn provided the Santa Fe for much of its repeat business. (RAILWAY AGE, May 20, 1963)

The Santa Fe began a program of cutting passenger fares by 20% in 1964. One example were the Chicago - Dallas round trip fares:

Type	Previous	20% Cut	Air Fare	Bus Fare
Coach	$52.80	$41.10	$94.50	$41.50
First Class	$66.65	$51.85		

The Santa Fe was truly the "Way to Go All the Way." The company, with its positive marketing and operations philosophy, also went "All the Way" with its publicity programs. Which, incidentally, portrayed what was really happening on the railroad. This publicity scene of a line up of passenger trains was taken at Chicago with a mixture of the early diesel power and the streamlined steam power taking center stage. This photo goes back to the early part of the "Streamlined Era" with the trains left to right, The *Super Chief*, the *El Capitan*, the 2nd *Super Chief*, the *Chief*, the 2nd *Chief* and the 2nd *El Capitan*. The new streamlined *Super Chief* and *El Capitan* were not yet on a daily schedule between Chicago and Los Angeles. (Santa Fe Railway Photo, Harry Stegmaier Collection)

Santa Fe passenger train services always had a sense of romance and beauty regardless of the era of being portrayed. Double-header steam power on passenger trains were very common throughout the steam era right into the "Streamlined Era." In this case, an All-Pullman train is rounding a curve near Flagstaff, Arizona. (Santa Fe Railway Photo, Kansas State Historical Society Collection)

The primary traffic was the automobile traveler, but the new rates were below both air coach and bus fares on many routes. The fare reductions were largely in effect from September 15th through April 30 for the off-seasons. Santa Fe's peak season travel meanwhile continued to do well. For example, passenger counts on the transcontinental trains in 1964 was 8% higher during the summer of 1964 compared to the summer of 1963.

The Santa Fe continued its program for keeping passengers on board. The railroad continually held meetings with employees for ideas, suggestions, and to define problem areas. By 1965, the railroad had been holding such positive working meetings for over 20 years. The positive attitude with employees always resulted in strengthening the overall profit picture. This also brought about a positive working relationship with the Unions. The employees were encouraged to give ideas and talk, and could do so without getting into deep difficulties. As the General Passenger Traffic Manager Chappel pointed out in a 1965, "You, out there on the line, can see things that we can't always see back at headquarters." (RAILWAY AGE, March 8, 1965, p. 21.)

Moving into the late 1960s, as everyone knows, things became more difficult. However, the attitude on the Santa Fe continued to be very positive. The railroad launched a one-price ticket program, which included coach, meals, and Pullman or seat services. The program was started as a result of a marketing research project, which indicated that passengers preferred a ticket of this type. The fare reductions of 20% continued between September 15 and May 15 as of 1968.

The year 1967 did not turn out to be a good one exactly. Passenger revenues dropped over 17% in 1967 com-

pared to 1966. Part of the problem was the loss of the Railway Post Office services and new reduced rates for handling bulk mail. As 1967 drew to a close, the Santa Fe's preliminary plan was to drop most of the passenger services with the exception of the *Super Chief*, the *El Capitan*, the *San Francisco Chief* and *Texas Chief* as well as the remaining *San Diegans*. The Santa Fe had done much to retain and grow the passenger traffic levels over the years, but as the 1960s rolled on, the automobile and air line traffic continued to increase in unprecedented amounts. Just one example of the air traffic were 165 scheduled daily flights between Chicago and California alone.

Thus as 1967 drew to a close, the Santa Fe petitioned to discontinue 12 sets of trains including the *Grand Canyon* and the *Chief*. This would have left the four trains listed above plus the *San Diegans* in service on one of the most positive passenger train service operators - the Santa Fe. Two of the first sets of trains to be dropped in October, 1967 were trains 7 and 8, the *Fast Mail* between Chicago and Los Angeles; and trains 3 and 4 between Kansas City and Gallup, New Mexico.

Trains 3 and 4 was coach only and provided a further west connection from overnight train No. 9 (The *Kansas City Chief*), and for the overnight operation of the *Chief*, train 20 from Kansas City to Chicago. Trains 7 and 8 handled mail traffic only.

In December of 1967, the Santa Fe sought to discontinue the *Grand Canyon* and the *Chief* as quickly as possible. The loss of the mail traffic alone resulted in drops of revenue of over $5.5 million for the two trains between 1966 and 1967. Passenger patronage was also dropping. The ICC denied permission to discontinue the two sets of trains between Chicago and Los Angeles. Eventually, by 1969, the *Chief* was discontinued, but the remains of the *Grand Canyon*, trains 23 and 24 continued in operation.

During the final full year of Santa Fe passenger train operations through 1970 up to May, 1971, the company operated four sets of transcontinental trains:

* The combined *Super Chief* and *El Capitan*
* The *San Francisco Chief*
* Trains 23 and 24, the former *Grand Canyon*.

The *Texas Chief*, trains 15 and 16 continued to provide Chicago and Texas service. A secondary schedule was provided in part by trains 23 and 24, which connected with trains 211 and 212, the *Tulsan*, for service between Kansas City and Tulsa. The only other existing connecting train service was the pair 201-200 and 191-190 between La Junta and Denver. Technically, the train only provided a decent connection on the run from Denver to La Junta to connect with eastbound train 18, the combined *Super Chief* and *El Capitan*. Westbound connections at La Junta from train 17 meant an eleven hour wait for the train to travel to Denver. Since this was not practical, the Santa Fe did provided connections with a bus for both train 23 and 17 to give passengers a decent arrival in Denver.

There were still three *San Diegans* each way between Los Angeles and San Diego but that was it!

When Amtrak began service on the Santa Fe in May, 1971, there was but two trains remaining, the *Texas Chief* and the Chicago - LA operations, which were designated trains 15 and 16, The *Texas Chief*; and 17 and 18 the combined *Super Chief* and the *El Capitan*. This would soon change as time went. Refer to Chapter 12 regarding Amtrak services on the Santa Fe.

There is no doubt about it, the Santa Fe operated one of the best passenger systems in North America. The clean trains, appropriately scheduled, and positive working relationships with staffs and train crews provides a base line for an even greater knowledge base in the 21st Century on how to operate a transportation system. In fact, really, for any type of an organization designed to provide services to vast array of clients, passengers, freight shippers and students and families. The Santa Fe was a prime example of a superb Service Organization. As mentionedabove, there is no doubt about it, the Santa Fe was the way to go - All the way!

We have to go back in history a bit to illustrate at least one early 20th Centu passenger power. This 4-4-0 steam engine, the 48, is heading up a passe ger at San Diego in May, 1911. Who could have known that over 90 yea later, the route to San Diego would be handling over 40 passenger trains a da with Amtrak and the Coaster Commuter Services, a subject covered later this book. (Harold K. Vollrath Collection)

Oil Burning Pacific No. 3448 is heading up a consist of 10 cars and is passing Mile Post 9 just west of Chicago. Note the farm fields in the background. This is a typical example of a train during the late 1930s and into the 1940s with steam power, heavyweight equipment during the beginning of the "Streamlined Era." (Santa Fe Railway Photo)

This photo dates back to 1936 with an arrival at Dallas, Texas of a steam powered passenger train with the 1228 doing the honors. Note the Pullman cars ahead of the head-end cars in the consist of this particular train. The sleepers were being transferred for still another service, of which the details are now no longer known. (Harold K. Vollrath Collection)

Pullman Sleeping Car accommodations ranged from open sections (upper and lower berths), to roomettes, compartments, drawing rooms and double bedrooms with a variety of seating and comfortable beds. This photo illustrates the interior of a drawing room, which could accommodate 3 adult passengers with a sofa bed and an upper and lower berth. (Santa Fe Railway Photo, Harry Stegmaier Collection)

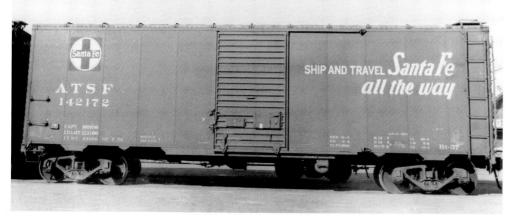

The Santa Fe provided "Rolling Information" systems with advertising on the railroad box cars. Forty foot, single door car No. 142172 illustrates the "Ship and Travel SANTA FE all the way," which was common for one side of the cars. The opposite side advertised specific trains. For other box car photos refer to Chapters 2 and 3. (Photo by W. C. Whittaker)

This photo depicts the Santa Fe philosophy for a friendly and helpful approach as a car attendant assists a couple with their suitcases while boarding a Pullman car on the *Super Chief.* (Santa Fe Railway photo)

SANTA FE SYSTEM LINES
Serving the West and Southwest

These Famous Santa Fe Trains
to Serve You on your Vacation This Summer

THE SUPER CHIEF—America's most preferred all-first-class streamliner between Chicago and Los Angeles.

THE CHIEF—Famous daily all-first-class streamliner serving the Southwest and California.

EL CAPITAN — the extra fare, all-chair-car transcontinental streamliner that made railroad history.

THE CALIFORNIA LIMITED and THE GRAND CANYON LIMITED—providing daily service between Chicago and the West.

THE SCOUT — Famous economy train for points between Chicago and California — helps you stretch that vacation budget.

Still another facet of travel on the Santa Fe were the Indian Guides who provid a wealth of information for travelers throughout the Southwest. The guid dressed in full tribal costume and rode the Santa Fe's eastbound *Super Chief* a the westbound *El Capitan* to explain to passengers the various landmarks, his ry and other colorful sights of the Southwest. In this photo, Santa Fe Guide Ha Nieto is in the Pleasure Dome of the *Super Chief* explaining to passengers famous Red Cliffs which the train passes near Gallup. This added another dim sion for Travel on the Santa Fe All the Way. (Santa Fe Railway Photo, Kans State Historical Society Collection)

Santa Fe

Santa Fe all the way

11

PASSENGER TRAFFIC LEVELS
LATE 1920s to AMTRAK

YEAR	NUMBER PASSENGERS CARRIED	AVERAGE MILES PER PASSENGER	YEAR	NUMBER PASSENGERS CARRIED	AVERAGE MILES PER PASSENGER
28	4,520,339	272.2	1951	3,930,779	562.1
29	4,253,695	291.6	1952	4,247,660	565.4
30	3,274,826	320.7	1953	3,693,406	564.5
			1954	3,445,168	565.5
31	2,287,747	349.3	1955	3,404,739	570.7
32	1,619,428	354.2	1956	3,192,474	620.4
33	1,362,028	407.4	1957	2,821,540	629.1
34	1,864,091	342.8	1958	2,678,033	621.7
35	2,263,197	330.5	1959	2,621,223	639.0
36	2,489,949	350.5	1960	2,525,947	668.7
37	2,645,221	370.5			
38	2,336,295	390.4	1961	2,444,562	693.7
39	2,595,556	398.1	1962	2,432,501	698.3
40	2,707,306	390.1	1963	2,370,270	682.2
			1964	2,496,063	682.9
41	3,192,993	415.1	1965	2,317,443	713.2
42	6,457,914	466.7	1966	2,378,275	706.1
43	10,399,212	560.3	1967	2,132,752	671.2
44	11,263,992	554.8	1968	1,504,739	657.9
45	10,277,575	619.5	1969	1,304,162	652.4
46	6,844,776	587.8	1970	1,197,996	606.9
47	5,059,039	469.1			
48	4,584,607	493.7	1971	339,443	481.2
49	4,096,740	498.1			
50	3,615,519	520.2			

Note: Amtrak began passenger operations on May 1, 1971. If the Santa Fe had continued the rate of passenger patronage it had for the first four months of 1971, the company could have achieved an annual number of 1,018,329 simply based on the earlier patronage figures. However, the first four months of the year is generally the lowest travel period. Had the Santa Fe continued through the Summer and into the Holiday Season of 1971, the passenger patronage for 1971 had the potential for an increase over the 1970 figures.

Santa Fe passenger trains can be modeled quite easily, especially with the new Walther's Santa Fe passenger equipment and motive power currently (2004) being produced. Walthers produces a variety of streamlined equipment for the *Super Chief* as well as coach equipment which are exact for the Santa Fe. The model equipment includes:

Budd 73' Baggage Car 3500 Series
Budd 63' Railway Post Office Car, 89 to 98 Series
Budd 46 Seat Coach without skirts
Pullman-Standard 36 Seat Dining Car
Pullman-Standard 29 Seat Dormitory Lounge Car
Budd Pine Series 10 Roomette, 6 Double Bedroom Sleeping Car
Pullman-Standard Cascade Series 10 Roomette, 5 Double Bedroom Sleeping Car
Pullman-Standard 4 Compartment, 4 Double Bedroom and 2 Drawing Room Car,
Such as the Tsankawi.
Budd Dome Lounge Car, Pleasure Dome
Observation Car, Vista Series

Three of the models are illustrated here:

Baggage Car No. 3500

Rail Post Office Car No. 90

The 4 Compartment, 4 Double Bedroom, 2 Drawing Room Car, the Tsankawi

(All Photos are Walthers)

Chapter 2 - THE ROUTE OF "CHIEFS" AND "EL CAPITAN"

The Santa Fe operated a spectacular streamliner fleet between Chicago and the West Coast as well as Texas. The streamliner era began on the Santa Fe during the Great Depression, and was part of their positive philosophy of working with staff and building markets for a solid traffic base. By the year 1940, the trains that had started out as weekly ventures were expanding the service levels to every other day and eventually to a daily basis. This chapter takes a look at the *Route of the Chiefs* which included the following trains that were developed during the late 1930s through the late 1940s:

> The Super Chief
> The El Capitan
> The Chief
> The Texas Chief
> The San Francisco Chief
> The Kansas City Chief

Many of the trains were Extra Fare trains, although this did change as the passenger history hi-balled through the 1960s. And to begin with, two of the transcontinental trains were All-Pullman and one was All-Coach. The *Super Chief*, the *Chief*, and the *El Capitan* played a role with these special type of services. The fleet was always fast, but even more important, provided reliable train services. Furthermore, the scheduling of the trains between Chicago and the West Coast was done in such a way to provide travelers with a chance to relax, enjoy the landscape, and have a chance to think.

Two nights and one day travel between Chicago and California is far more beneficial than rushing to an airport, waiting in lines for everything, and then scrambling for transportation at the end of the flight. What the Santa Fe provided for the transcontinental traveler, as well as the intermediate points with the *Chiefs*, are concepts that could be utilized as we move through the 21st Century.

THE SUPER CHIEF

The *Super Chief* was placed in service 1936. Originally, it was a once a week train with an All-Pullman consist. By 1940, the train was operating twice a week between Chicago and Los Angeles.

The 1940 time tables showed that the Super Chief, train 17, departed Chicago in the evenings on Tuesday and Saturday with an early arrival in LA on Thursday and Monday mornings respectively. The eastbound train 18 departed Los Angeles later in the evening with an arrival

two days later in Chicago before 2:00 p.m.

The consists of the bi-weekly trains included:

> 1 Club Baggage Car
> 3 Pullman Sleeping Cars
> 1 Club Lounge Car
> 1 Dining Car
> 2 Pullman Sleeping Cars
> 1 Sleeper Observation Car.

The trains were completely air-conditioned and included valet, maid, barber service, men's shower bath and radio plus daily market reports and news bulletins.

There was also maid and manicure services, women's shower and bath. The trains got off to a terrific start, and things were going to be even better in the future.

Rolling into 1946, the hectic traffic levels of World War II were coming to an end. The Santa Fe placed the *Super Chief* on an every other day schedule departing Chicago and Los Angeles on even-numbered days. (The *El Capitan* was operated on the odd numbered days.) The running time of 39 hours, 45 minutes continued.

February 29, 1948 was the date that the *Super Chief* began operating on a daily schedule between Chicago and Los Angeles. The schedule of 39 hours and 45 minutes continued in effect. The train was now an All-Room train with roomettes, bedroom-compartment suites, drawing rooms, as well as individual bedrooms and compartments. New passenger equipment made the new daily service possible, and there was no lack of patronage for the *Super Chief*.

The Santa Fe ordered dome lounge cars for the *Super Chief* in 1950. The cars went into service on January 28, 1951 making the *Super Chief* a Domeliner. The car included a room called the Turquoise Room, a lower level cocktail lounge area, the main lounge room, and the dome section.

The Turquoise Room was named after a Traveler's Stone of the Southwest, and was designed for dining and beverage service for private parties. It featured turquoise, silver and gold decor, accordian-type sliding doors, specially designed service plate to harmonize with the decorative treatment of the room and full color reproductions of various scenic areas in the Southwest. The dome featured revolving type chairs. The dome lounge car added an entire new concept of travel for the All-Pullman *Super Chief*.

The year 1951 saw additional enhancements for the

Equipment listings for the transcontinental trains including the Super Chief, El Capitan, the Chief, and San Francisco Chief. For the Texas Chief schedule, see Chapter 3 in a combined timetable. (Spring, 1960 Timetable)

charge for the *Super Chief* was reduced from $15 to $7.50 in late 1953.

The configuration of the *Super Chief* changed by 1960. For example, since 1958 during the off seasons, the *Super Chief* and the *El Capitan* operated together as one train, numbers 17 and 18. However, the two trains were still two separate groups even though running in one train. The 1960 consist included:

1 Baggage Dormitory Car
3 Sleeping Cars Chicago - Los
    Angeles
1 Dome Lounge Car
1 Dining Car
1 Sleeping Car Chicago - Los
    Angeles
1 Sleeping Car Kansas City - Los
    Angeles

During the period June 9th through September 12 in 1960, the Santa Fe also operated Chair Cars within the consist of the *Super Chief*. Also during this period of time the *El Capitan* and *Super Chief* operated separately as two sections of trains 17 and 18 in both directions.

Business continued to flourish on the *Super Chief*. For example, in 1961, the Santa Fe saw an increase of 43% in advance reservations as compared with 1960. In fact, reservations had increased on all of the Santa Fe trains that year. It was but another example of the positive marketing program, the high standards of passenger service, and a willingness of the company to look at different options for service - to fulfill the needs of the traveling public.

New sleeping cars came to the *Super Chief* in 1964. The Santa Fe obtained 12 new 11 Double Bedroom from the Pullman Shops in Chicago. The cars had been completely rebuilt from the frame up. The first run of the new equipment took place in May, 1964. Two of the new cars were assigned to each train's consist on a daily basis.

The summer season consist of the *Super Chief* continued to prosper. For example, in 1966 the train operated with 6 sleeping cars. Five were Chicago and Los Angeles, while one was the Kansas City - LA assignment. The train continued to operate with the dome lounge car and the dining car. However, what is interesting is the inclusion of 5 Chair Cars in each direction between Chicago and Los Angeles as well as dining car and lounge car for the Coach passengers. As was normal, the *El Capitan* and *Super Chief* ran separately as 1st and 2nd 17 and 18 during the heavy traffic periods of time.

Super Chief. The railroad had ordered three types of cars from American Car and Foundry Co. It added to the travel convenience and pleasure for the All-Pullman train.

A new Observation/Lounge/Sleeping car with four drawing rooms and one double bedroom graced the rear of the train. The lounge section consisted of a 24 foot area with 12 lounge chairs. The chairs were placed six to each side of the car toward the rounded end of the equipment.

One of the two sets of full Sleeping cars was the 10 roomette, 6 double bedroom type. Thirteen cars of this group were ordered. The 10-6 style provided sleeping accommodations for a total of 22 people. Each pair of bedrooms had a folding partition so that the two rooms could be made en suite if passengers desired. It was an excellent system for family travel. The third set of new equipment consisted of four double bedrooms, four compartments and two drawing rooms with accommodations for 22 passengers. The three sets of equipment went into service upon delivery in 1951.

The *Super Chief* continued to operate on its fast schedule into the 1950s. One of the changes was the Extra Fare

Chicago and California
(Via Amarillo and Belen)

Read down						Read up	
No. 3 Daily	No. 1 Daily	Miles	Table **7**		No. 2 Daily		No. 4 Daily
AM	PM		*Central Standard Time*		PM		PM
....	3.15	.0	Lv....CHICAGO....Ar		2.00		....
....	10.30	451.1	Ar...Kansas City....Lv		6.30		....
9.15	10.39	451.1	Lv...Kansas City....Ar		6.00		3.00
....	10.50	451.1	Lv...Kansas City....Ar		6.00		....
....	11.55	516.9	"....Topeka.... "		4.25		....
12.25	2.20	636.2	Ar....Newton....Lv		2.05		11.05
12.35	2.25	636.2	"....Newton.... "		1.50		10.50
1.15	3.10	663.4	"....Wichita.... "		1.10		9.55
2.00	3.55	697.5	Ar....WELLINGTON....Lv		12.20		9.10
2.05	4.00	697.5	Lv.WELLINGTON 28, 64.Ar		12.15		9.05
....	f4.34	732.4	"....Harper 31.... "		f11.30		....
....	....	738.9	"....Eula.... "		....		....
....	f4.48	744.2	"....Attica 34.... "		f11.14		....
....	5.15	765.5	"...Kiowa, Kan.... "		10.50		....
....	....	775.0	"..Capron, Okla.... "		....		f7.45
3.22	5.34	783.3	"....Alva.... "		10.27		f7.36
....	....	794.3	"....Avard.... "		....		f7.22
3.50	6.05	804.1	"...WAYNOKA 40a... "		10.05		7.10
....	....	806.9	*Cimarron River*				....
....	f6.18	819.5	"....Quinlan.... "		f9.31		....
....	f6.27	829.6	"....Mooreland.... "		f9.21		....
4.26	6.38	840.2	"....Woodward.... "		9.12		6.05
....	6.56	855.7	"....Fargo.... "		f8.50		....
5.00	7.13	864.1	"....Gage.... "		f8.41		5.29
....	....	871.8	"..Shattuck 81 Okla.... "		8.30		....
			Texas State Line P.&S.F. Ry.				
....	7.28	886.1	Lv..Higgins, Tex....Ar		f8.12		....
....	f7.42	901.4	"....Glazier....Lv		....		....
		910.9	*South Canadian River*				
5.40	7.54	912.5	"....Canadian.... "		7.45		4.45
6.02	f8.20	934.3	"....Miami.... "		f7.21		....
6.29	8.52	956.3	"....Pampa 82.... "		6.59		3.53
....	f9.00	963.3	"...Kingsmill.... "		f6.46		....
....	f9.09	970.2	"...White Deer.... "		f6.35		....
....	f9.21	983.4	"..Panhandle 84.... "		f6.25		....
7.30	10.00	1010.4	Ar..AMARILLO 4, 46, 79.Lv		6.10		2.55
....	10.35	.0	Lv....Amarillo....Ar		5.25		....
....	12.59	121.6	Ar....Lubbock....Lv		3.05		....
7.50	10.10	1010.4	Lv....AMARILLO....Ar		6.00		2.40
....	f10.30	1027.8	"....Canyon 79....Lv		5.38		....
....	11.03	1056.9	"....Hereford.... "		5.12		....
....	f11.30	1079.2	"....Friona.... "		4.52		....
....	f11.45	1091.5	"....Bovina.... "		f4.42		....
....	f11.59	1104.8	Ar.Farwell-Texico 10a Tex.Lv		f4.31		....
			Texas-N. M. State Line				
9.30	12.15	1114.1	Ar.CLOVIS 10a 79a 80 N Mex.Lv		4.20		12.55
....	1.45	1114.1	Lv..CLOVIS (M.S.T.)....Ar		1.00		....
....	6.00	1297.8	Ar....Carlsbad....Lv		8.45		....
			Mountain Standard Time				
8.40	11.50	1114.1	Lv...CLOVIS....Ar		2.45		11.45
....	..b..	1174.2	"..Ft. Sumner.... "		..k..		....
		1175.9	*Pecos River*				
10.40	1.50	1244.9	"....Vaughn....Lv		12.45		9.33
....	f3.00	1313.1	"....Mountainair.... "		f11.47		....
12.40	3.50	1353.9	Ar..BELEN 4, 9a, 10a....Lv		11.00		7.40
....	4.00	1353.9	Lv....Belen....Ar		10.50		....
....	4.55	1384.1	Ar...Albuquerque....Lv		9.50		....
....	2.50	0.0	Lv...Albuquerque....Ar		11.55		....
....	3.50	30.2	Lv....Belen.... "		11.00		....
....	4.00	1353.9	Lv....Belen....Ar		10.50		7.30
12.55	6.10	1497.9	Ar....Gallup....Lv		8.38		5.15
3.15	6.12	1497.9	"....Gallup.... "		8.35		....
....	7.54	1625.3	Ar....Winslow....Lv		6.50		....

No. 123	No. 1				No. 2	No. 124
9.50	8.00	1625.5	Lv....Winslow....Ar	6.45	4.40
12.05	9.44	1718.9	Ar....Williams....Lv	5.12	2.35
....	....	1718.9	"....Williams....Lv	10.20	....
4.15	7.00	1783.2	"...Grand Canyon....Lv	8.00	....
8.20	9.25	64.3	Lv...Grand Canyon....Ar	7.00	....
12.05	9.44	1718.9	"....Williams....Lv	4.15	2.35
1.07	10.40	1741.9	Ar....Ash Fork....Lv	4.25	1.30
2.10	....	0	Lv....Ash Fork....Ar	10.15	....
8.30	....	193.7	Ar....Phoenix....Lv	4.00	1.00
1.07	10.40	1741.9	Lv....Ash Fork....Ar	4.25	1.30
7.30	3.45	2085.9	Ar..Barstow (P.S.T.)..Lv	9.20	5.35
7.45	....	2085.9	Lv....Barstow....Ar		5.25
9.55	....	2166.0	Ar..San Bernardino...Lv		3.13
10.25	....	2176.0	"....Riverside....Lv		2.40
12.10	....	2223.7	Ar...LOS ANGELES...Lv		1.15

No. 74					No. 73
1.30	....	0	Lv...LOS ANGELES...Ar	10.15
4.15	....	127.0	Ar....San Diego....Lv	7.30
7.45	3.55	2085.9	Lv....Barstow....Ar	9.10	4.35
10.45	7.20	2226.9	Ar...Bakersfield....Lv	5.30	1.25
2.30	7.45	2226.9	Lv...Bakersfield....Lv	5.25	1.10

Motor Coach	Motor Coach				Motor Coach	Motor Coach
8.40	2.15	2546.7	Ar.SAN FRANCISCO...Lv	11.15	7.00
PM	PM		*Pacific Standard Time*	AM	AM

shown in dark figures indicates p.m.

The *San Francisco Chief* operated between Chicago and Richmond with bus connections to San Francisco. This particular timetable shows how the *San Francisco Chief* served a variety of points via Amarillo and Belen along with a secondary train. (Spring, 1960 Timetable)

It is a bit hard to believe that in 1966, Amtrak was but five years away. However, the Santa Fe continued to maintain superb passenger train standards on the *Super Chief*, and in fact, all of the passenger services. The 1969 time tables listed the *Super Chief* as All Private Room Sleeping Car Service and continued to operate sleeping cars for Chicago - Los Angeles and Kansas City - Los Angeles. The Dome Lounge car and Dining Car were still an important part of the train's services for passengers. No. 17 departed Chicago at 6:30 p.m. with a 9:00 a.m. arrival in LA the second morning. Eastbound No. 18 departed LA at 7:30 p.m. with a 1:30 p.m. arrival in Chicago on the second day.

The *Super Chief* was selected as one of Amtrak's trains in 1971. This brought an end to the era of the Santa Fe "Super Chief", which is a prime example of what passenger service can be for transcontinental operations. There is much to learn from the Santa Fe. Furthermore, the *Super Chief* was not the only superb train to be in operation between Chicago and the West Coast. Its prime companion train was the *El Capitan*, the next section of this chapter.

THE EL CAPITAN

The *El Capitan* began service in 1938, the year following the *Super Chief*. It began service with a twice weekly operation between Chicago and Los Angeles. The *El Capitan* was still providing twice weekly service in 1940 and running as trains 21 and 22. The train departed Chicago at 5:45 p.m. with a 7:30 a.m. arrival in Los Angeles on the second morning. Train 22 departed LA at 1:30 p.m. with a 7:15 a.m. arrival in Chicago. 21 and 22 departed both LA and Chicago on Tuesdays and Saturdays during the early part of its career.

The *El Capitan's* services included a Courier-Nurse, free pillows and drinking cups, and porter service. The train operated with a Baggage-Chair Car, and several Delux Chair Cars. Meal and beverage service was provided with a Lunch-Counter Dining Car, which served all meals. Breakfast prices ranged from 40 to 75 cents, lunches from 50 to 80 cents, and dinners from 65 to a $1.00. A la carte services were also available for passengers.

The frequency of service was increased to tri-weekly in 1941. However, the history of the *El Capitan* was going to expand substantially after World War II. In 1946, the train was re equipped and placed on an every other day schedule in both directions. The *El Capitan*, being the running mate of the *Super Chief*, departed Chicago and LA on odd-numbered days. The train did not operate on the 31st of any month. The overall schedule of under 40 hours continued.

The Courier-nurse service, provided for traveling mothers and babies, children traveling alone and for the ill, invalids and aged had been discontinued during the War Years. The railroad reestablished the service in early 1947. Twenty six registered nurses were employed for the service for both the *El Capitan* and the *Scout*. The group completed a training program about the railroad and train schedules including tours of the line to bring up the knowledge levels of travel attractions and the important train services.

The *El Capitan* began a new daily service routine on February 28, 1948 along with the *Super Chief*. New equipment provided the railroad with the opportunity to expand service for several train operations, and to continue the fast 39 hour, 45 minute schedules between Chicago and LA.

The 1948 schedules show that the All-Coach Extra Fare *El Capitan* departed Chicago at 5:45 p.m. with its 7:30 a.m. arrival in LA; and a 1:30 p.m. departure from Los Angeles and 7:15 a.m. arrival in Chicago - the second day. The new coaches for the service were built by Pullman-Standard with the exception of new Lunch-Counter Diners,

Chicago and Kansas City (For other service, see Table 1, pages 16 & 17)

WEST—Read down   EAST—Read up

No. 9 Kansas City Chief	Daily Example	Mls.	Table JJ	No. 10 Kansas City Chief	Daily Example
10.00PM	Sunday	0	Lv....Chicago (C.S.T.)....Ar	7.30AM	Monday
10.55PM	"	38	"......Joliet........Lv	6.30AM	"
11.50PM	"	90	"......Streator......."	5.25AM	"
12.15AM	Monday	110	"......Toluca......."	....	"
12.40AM	"	130	"......Chillicothe......."	4.40AM	"
1.45AM	"	178	"......Galesburg......."	3.40AM	"
2.55AM	"	233	"......Ft. Madison......."	2.40AM	"
3.05AM	"	235	"......Shopton......."	2.30AM	"
4.40AM	"	313	"......La Plata......."	12.50AM	"
5.20AM	"	347	"......Marceline......."	12.10AM	"
6.05AM	"	386	"......Carrollton......"	11.20PM	Sunday
7.45AM	"	451	Ar......Kansas City......Lv	10.00PM	"

Equipment

Trains 9 and 10 between Chicago and Kansas City.

Lounge Car	Chicago and Kansas City.
Sleeping Car	Chicago and Kansas City—10 Roomette, 6 D. B. R.
	Chicago and Kansas City—24 Duplex Roomette.
	Chicago and Kansas City—10 Roomette, 5 D. B. R.
	Chicago and Kansas City—6 Roomette, 6 Sec., 4 D. B. R.
	Chicago and Kansas City—17 Roomette.
Lunch-Counter Diner	Chicago and Kansas City.
Chair Car	Chicago and Kansas City.

Chicago and Kansas City

For other service, see Table 1, pages 16 & 17

WEST—Read down   EAST—Read up

No. 9 Kansas City Chief	Daily Example	Mls.	Table E	No. 20 The Chief	Daily Example
			Central Standard Time		
10.00PM	Sunday	0	Lv....Chicago........Ar	7.15AM	Monday
10.50PM	"	38	"......Joliet........Lv	6.10AM	"
11.12PM	"	59	"......Coal City......."	....	
11.50PM	"	90	"......Streator......."	5.15AM	"
12.15AM	Monday	110	"......Toluca......."	dd4.54AM	"
12.45AM	"	130	"......Chillicothe......."	4.35AM	"
1.35AM	"	178	"......Galesburg......."	3.45AM	"
2.45AM	"	233	"......Ft. Madison......."	2.55AM	"
2.55AM	"	235	"......Shopton......."	2.50AM	"
4.20AM	"	313	"......La Plata......."	dd1.26AM	"
5.00AM	"	347	"......Marceline......."	....	
5.37AM	"	386	"......Carrollton......"	....	
6.00AM	"	411	"......Henrietta......."	....	
7.00AM	"	451	Ar......Kansas City......Lv	11.00PM	Sunday

Equipment

Trains 9 and 20 between Chicago and Kansas City.

Lounge Car	Chicago and Kansas City.
Sleeping Car	Chicago and Kansas City—10 Roomette, 5 D. B. R.
	Chicago and Kansas City—10 Roomette, 6 D. B. R.
Dining Car	Kansas City to Chicago (Fred Harvey Service).
Chair Car	Chicago and Kansas City.

These two timetables and equipment lists for the *Kansas City Chief* illustrate the changes that took place between 1954 and 1960. Table JJ shows the schedule and the equipment for 1954, while Table E shows the longer running time of No. 9, fewer sleeping cars, and the combination with the eastbound *Chief* No. 20 in 1960. (Jan., 1954 and Spring, 1960 Timetables)

which had been built by the Budd Company.

More new equipment for the *El Capitan* was on the way by the early 1950s. In fact, the *El Capitan* could be regarded as one of the few trains that received a wide variety of new equipment during its career with some very interesting innovations. For example, the Santa Fe ordered eight full length dome lounge cars from the Budd Company, five of which were assigned to the *El Capitan*. The area below the dome included a nurse's room and a 28 seat cocktail lounge decorated with Native American symbols and art work.

Each dome car provided seating for 103 passengers. Angled seats in the dome seated 57 passengers. The upper deck lounge area provided seats for 18 passengers. Twenty eight people could enjoy the club lounge section on the lower level. The full length dome cars inspired the Santa Fe to look at some other innovative ideas for new Chair Cars.

Moving forward to 1954, and the Santa Fe added a new system of low price "budget" means on the *El Capitan*. But that is only part of the big story beginning in 1954.

The Santa Fe designed and worked with the Budd Company to create a new concept in long distance coach design with two experimental "Hi-level" Chair Cars. The cars were double deck cars with all coach seating for 67 passengers on the upper level. The cars had the same space between seats as did the 44/48 seat, leg-rest reclining seat Chair cars. The lower level contained the car entrance, baggage space, rest rooms and service equipment, such as the air condition equipment.

The cars were 15 feet high and 85 feet long. The two cars were operated on an experimental basis on the *El Capitan* in 1954. The results of the research, including passenger reactions and thoughts, brought about an order of 47 Hi-level passenger equipment from the Budd Company. The order included 35 Chair Cars, 6 Dining Cars, and 6 lounge cars with more window areas including the top of the

car. Delivery took place in 1956 making the *El Capitan* a full Hi-level train.

The new Hi-level Dining cars provided seating for 80 passengers with the kitchen located on the lower level. Food was transported to the upper level by two elevators. The Hi-level Lounge cars provided seating for 88 passengers. Lounge seating was available on both levels. The lower level included a newsstand, serving bar and rest rooms. The Hi-level Lounge car was designated the Sky Lounge car.

The new *El Capitan* was decorated with Southwest Native American Art. The cars were also equipped with a public address system carrying recorded music, radio programs, and train announcements. The reequipped *El Capitan* operated with 7 Chair Cars plus the dining and lounge cars. The seven Chair cars provided seating for 496 passengers as compared to the 350 passenger seating in eight single level coaches.

The regular assigned consist of the new *El Capitan* looked like this in 1956:

1 Storage Mail Car
1 Baggage Car
1 Dormitory Baggage Car with modified roof
to match the Hi-level cars.
1 68 Passenger Hi-level Coach
2 72 Passenger Hi-level Coaches
1 Hi-level Dining Car
1 Sky Lounge Car
3 72 Passenger Hi-level Coaches
1 68 Passenger HI-level Coach

The *El Capitan* was combined with the *Super Chief* in 1958 and assumed the *Chief's* train numbers, 17 and 18. The 1960 Edition of the *El Capitan* departed Chicago at 6:30 p.m. with an arrival in Los Angeles at 8:00 a.m. the

The eastbound *Super Chief* is climbing Raton Pass just below Wooten, Colorado with two E units for power for a total of 4000 horsepower, which means a helper s needed. Santa Fe's big 2-10-4, No. 5000 is doing the honors in helper service or the *Super Chief* with a grand display of the power and romance in railroading. Santa Fe Railway, Kansas State Historical Society Collection)

second morning. Eastbound 18 departed LA 8:00 p.m. with a 1:30 p.m. arrival in Chicago the second day. As mentioned previously, the trains ran as two sections during the summer seasons and the Holiday Seasons.

The Santa Fe's experience with the Hi-level Chair cars led to an order for 24 new 72 seat Hi-level cars from the Budd Company in 1962. The new cars arrived in 1964 and were assigned to the *El Capitan*, with the older equipment being assigned to the *San Francisco Chief*.

The *El Capitan* continued to run with its team mate, the *Super Chief*, until Amtrak day in 1971. What is interesting is that Amtrak took a second look at the Hi-level cars, which in turn led to the design of the Superliner Bi-level cars. Which incidentally, operate on the *Southwest Chief*.

There is no doubt about it, the El Capitan was a superb train in every respect. It was truly one of the best ways to travel between Chicago and Southern California.

THE CHIEF

The Santa Fe operated several passenger trains daily between Chicago and Los Angeles. The *Chief's* heavy weight equipment was replaced in 1938 with streamlined cars. The 1940 consist of this superb transcontinental was as follows:

1 Club Baggage Car
1 17 Roomette Pullman Chicago - Los Angeles
1 2 Drawing Room, 4 Compartment, 4 Double
    Bedroom Chicago - LA
1 2 Drawing Room, 4 Compartment, 4 Double
    Bedroom Chicago - Phoenix
(Connected with 47 from Ash Fork, or 42 to
Ash Fork)
1 Club Lounge Car

1 Dining Car
1 2 Drawing Room, 4 Compartment, 4 Double
    Bedroom Chicago - LA
1 8 Section, 2 Compartments, 2 Double
    Bedroom Chicago - LA
1 Observation Lounge Sleeper, 4 Drawing
    Rooms, 1 Double Bedroom
    Chicago - LA

Train 19 departed Chicago on a daily basis at 12:01 p.m. with an 11:50 a.m. arrival in LA two mornings later. Train 20 departed LA 11:30 a.m. with an arrival in Chicago at 1:25 p.m. two days later.

Service was expanded in 1942 with some coast to coast sleeping car service between New York and Los Angeles with connections in Chicago with the New York Central and the Pennsylvania. New through sleeping car service was established between Chicago and San Diego on March 29, 1947. Eastbound services began on April 1st. Still other interesting changes were soon to take place.

Effective April 27, 1947, the *Chief* began operating from Chicago to Los Angeles in 46 hours, 30 minutes. This cut 90 minutes from the previous schedule. The eastbound No. 20 made the new run in 46 hours, with a 60 minute cut from the previous schedule. Train 19 departed Chicago at 1:30 p.m. with a 8:30 a.m. arrival in LA, while No. 20 departed LA at 12:30 p.m. and arrived in Chicago at 11:30 a.m. the second day at the end of 1947. The schedules were improved even more by 1953 with the All-Pullman *Chief* scheduled for 39 hours, 30 minutes westbound; and 39 hours, 45 minutes eastbound.

The *Chief* became a Domeliner in 1956 when the Dome Lounge cars were transferred from the *El Capitan* to trains 19 and 20. The *Chief* had also became a Pullman and Chair Car Streamliner operation in the mid-1950s.

The *Chief* provided a substantial amount of intermediate service on the Chicago - Los Angeles route. The train provided not only Chicago - Los Angeles sleeping car services; but also Tulsa to Chicago, Topeka to Chicago, and Kansas City to Chicago. Indeed, this involved 5 Pullman car runs alone in 1960. There were two Chicago - LA Pullman runs plus 3 Chair cars each way. The Chief also handled Denver - Los Angeles Pullman car operations as well as one Chair car each way.

The *Chief* continued in operation until 1968. During its last year of operation in 1967, trains 19 and 20 provided a two day and one night schedule from Chicago to Los Angeles. The *Chief* departed Chicago at 9:00 a.m., and arrived in LA at 11:55 p.m. the next evening. Eastbound No. 20 departed Los Angeles at 10:30 a.m. and arrived in Chicago at 7:15 a.m. two mornings later. In fact, No. 20 served as the eastbound overnight train service between Kansas City and Chicago, and was basically running mate for the westbound overnight *Kansas City Chief*.

Equipment for the Westbound *Chief* included 5 Chair Cars, a Big Dome lounge car, 3 Chicago - LA Sleeping Cars and a Dining Car while the eastbound also included a Kansas City and Tulsa to Chicago Sleeping Cars during the summer of 1967. In addition, the eastbound handled a Los Angeles to Chicago Sleeping Car which operated via the

ther view of train 18, the Super Chief, is rounding a curve near Ribera, New xico. The train has 5 F units for power and the Pleasure Dome Lounge is but cars back from the engine. (Santa Fe Railway, John Sward Collection)

Grand Canyon eastbound only. The car was handled by train 15 from Williams Junction to the Grand Canyon, with the return run on No. 14 to Williams Junction.

The eastbound *Chief* also connected with train 42 at Williams Junction for passengers from Phoenix. Thus trains 19 and 20 were what one could call a multiple service type of streamliner. The *Chief* was discontinued during the year 1968.

THE TEXAS CHIEF

The *Texas Chief* was the next "Chief" to go into operation on the Santa Fe on April 3,1948. It operated on a daily basis between Chicago and Galveston, Texas with a running time of 26 hours, 30 minutes westbound, and 26 hours, 45 minutes eastbound. From the late 1940s through to the early and mid-1950s, the *Texas Chief* basically provided an overnight service between Chicago - Fort Worth with a bus connection between Fort Worth and Dallas.

During the early 1950s, trains 15 and 16 operated with the following equipment line up:
1 Lounge Car Chicago - Galveston
2 Pullman Sleeping Cars Chicago - Galveston (24 Duplex Rmt. And 4 Cmpt. 4 Dble Bdrm, 2 DR)
1 Pullman Sleeping Car Chicago - Wichita (10 Rmt, 3 Dble Bdrm, 2 Cmpt.)
1 Pullman Sleeping Car Chicago - Oklahoma City (10 Rmt., 6 Dble Bdrm)
1 Pullman Sleeping Car Chicago - Tulsa (10 Rmt., 3 Dble Bdrm, 2 Cmpt.)
1 Dining Car Chicago - Galveston
5 Chair Cars Chicago - Galveston

The basic schedule was a departure from Chicago at 6:00 p.m. with a 12:55 p.m. arrival at Fort Worth and an 8:15 p.m. arrival at Galveston. Train 16 departed

Galveston at 6:45 a.m. with a 2:00 p.m. departure from Fort Worth and a 9:00 a.m. arrival in Chicago the next morning.

By 1960, the *Texas Chief* still departed Chicago at 6:00 p.m. with an arrival at Fort Worth the next day at 12:55 p.m. No. 15 continued on to Galveston with an arrival at 8:15 p.m. Returning No. 16 departed Galveston at 6:50 a.m. with a 2:00 p.m. departure from Fort Worth and a 9:00 a.m. arrival in Chicago the next morning. Trains 15 and 16 provided sleeping car service between Chicago, Fort Worth, Houston and Wichita. Lounge car service was available from Chicago to Galveston.

The *Texas Chief* also handled a sleeping car and a chair car between Chicago and Dallas. The through cars were handled by trains 115 and 116 between Gainesville and Dallas on a daily basis, which began on Dec. 5, 1955 using the new Dallas-Denton cut-off.

The *Texas Chief* began to suffer from drops in patronage as the 1960s rolled on. Service was discontinued between Houston and Galveston in 1967. The Gainesville - Dallas connection was discontinued in 1968 and replaced with a bus service connection. On the other hand, a Big Dome Lounge car was added to the train's consist in 1968.

The 1969 timetable listed No. 15 with a departure at 5:20 p.m. from Chicago and an arrival at Fort Worth at 1:20 p.m. and an 8:00 p.m. arrival at Houston. No. 16 departed Houston at 7:20 a.m., Fort Worth at 1:08 p.m. and arrived at Chicago at 9:15 a.m. the next morning. The Big Dome operated between Chicago and Houston as well as the

The All-Pullman *Super Chief* is running as 1st No. 17 in this photo of the 14 car consist climbing the grade of Raton Pass in Southern Colorado. (Santa Fe Railway, John Sward Collection)

Dining Car, Chair Cars and at least one Sleeping Car. Two other Sleeping cars operated between Chicago and Fort Worth and Chicago and Topeka.

The *Texas Chief* continued in operation through 1971, and was selected by Amtrak for the Chicago - Houston service. Initially, the *Texas Chief* continued to run as trains 15 and 16 and was equipped with the Dome Lounge, Chair Cars, Dining Car and a Sleeper between Chicago and Houston. No. 15 departed Chicago at 5:00 p.m. with an

The Pleasure Dome Lounge car was without doubt one of the best ways to watch the scenery while traveling between Chicago and Los Angeles. No. 17 is climbing the grade at Raton Pass. (Santa Fe Railway, John Sward Collection)

arrival at Houston the next day at 8:30 p.m. No. 16 departed Houston at 7:20 a.m. with the Chicago arrival at 10:00 a.m. the next day. Eventually, the Texas Chief was discontinued and Amtrak operated the Texas Eagle over the Missouri Pacific lines between Chicago and Texas via St. Louis. (Refer to Chapter 11, Amtrak)

THE KANSAS CITY CHIEF

The *Kansas City Chief* was placed in operation on April 2, 1950. It began a new overnight Chicago - Kansas City train service. The train was initially equipped with leg-rest Chair Cars, a lunch counter - dining car and 4 to 5 Pullman sleeping cars. Initially the *Kansas City Chief* operated in both directions as trains 9 and 10. Both trains departed Chicago and Kansas City at 10:00 p.m. in the early 1950s. No. 9 arrived at Kansas City at 7:45 a.m., while No. 10 arrived in Chicago at 7:30 a.m.

No. 10 was ultimately combined with the *Chief* in 1958. Thus, No. 20, which arrived in Kansas City at 10:35 p.m. (1960 Timetable), picked up three additional Pullman Sleeping cars for the Kansas City to Chicago sleeping car traffic. The *Chief* arrived in Chicago with a grand total of seven Pullman sleeping cars on a daily basis during the late 1950s and early 60s.

By the mid-1960s, the *Kansas City Chief*, train 9, offered Chair Car services, the Lounge car for snacks and beverages and a light breakfast with its 7 a.m. arrival, and two Pullman sleeping cars for the Chicago - Kansas City traffic. The two cars operated eastbound on Train 20, the Chief from Kansas City to Chicago.

The *Chief* was discontinued in 1968, and so was the *Kansas City Chief* westbound from Chicago to KC. Overnight train services were completely gone. The closest element of overnight service was the *Texas Chief*, No. 16, which departed Kansas City at 1:35 a.m. with a 9:15 a.m. arrival in Chicago. A major segment of the Santa Fe passenger services had disappeared.

THE SAN FRANCISCO CHIEF

The newest *Chief* of the Santa Fe streamliners was the *San Francisco Chief*, which began operation on June 6,

Rounding one of the curves of the double horseshoe curve near Ribera, New Mexico is the Domeliner All-Coach *El Capitan*. The pre Hi-Level *El Capitan* was also equipped with a "Big Dome Lounge Car" until the new equipment arrived in 1956. The *El Capitan*, which was a running mate for the *Super Chief*, was always a favorite with the traveling public. The train operated as numbers 21 and 22 until combined with the *Super Chief*. (Santa Fe Railway, Patrick C. Dorin Collection)

El Capitan also ran in two sections, such as illustrated previously with the [Sup]*er Chief*. Note the green flags on the power. The green flags was an indica-[tion t]hat there was a following section. (White flags signified an "Extra Train" with[out] a time table schedule.) The *El Capitan* is shown here at Palmer Lake, [Colo]rado with 14 cars and running at 50 miles per hour on this July, 1951 sun-day. (Harold K. Vollrath Collection)

1954. The new train was actually a Domeliner with a full length dome lounge car as part of the consist of Chair Cars, Dining Car, and several Pullman Sleeping Cars. The new train enhanced the previous through car service operated with a series of connecting trains between Chicago and the San Francisco Bay Area. The new Chief also handled Pullman cars from Chicago to Phoenix, and also between New Orleans and Oakland with a Missouri Pacific connection. A through coach also provided a Houston - Oakland service.

The westbound *San Francisco Chief*, train No. 1, departed Chicago at 4:00 p.m. and arrived at Oakland in 1:10 p.m. on the second day. Eastbound No. 2 departed Oakland at 11:25 a.m. with an arrival at Chicago at 12:20 p.m., the second day. The running time was 47 hours, 10 minutes westbound, and 46 hours, 55 minutes eastbound for the 2,540.2 mile route between Chicago and Oakland.

The initial consist of the train included: (RAILWAY AGE, June 7, 1954)

1 Mail Storage Car   Kansas City - Oakland
1 Baggage, Mail and Express Chicago - Oakland
1 10 Roomette, 3 Dbrm., 2 Compt. Chicago -Phoenix
1 Lunch-counter Diner Dormitory Chicago - Oakland
3 Chair Cars Chicago - Oakland
1 Dining Car Chicago - Oakland
1 Big Dome Lounge Car Chicago - Oakland
2 Sleeping Cars Chicago - Oakland
    24 Duplex Roomette
    2 DR., 4 Compt., 4 Dbrm.
1 8 Section, 2 Compt., 2 Dbrm. New Orleans - Oakland
1 10 Roomette, 6 Dbrm. Kansas City - Oakland

The Santa Fe continued to make various adjustments for the *San Francisco Chief* as time went on. One example in 1957 was the unloading of passengers' checked luggage at Richmond and trucked downtown to San Francisco while the train finished its last 11 miles between Richmond and Oakland. When the passengers changed from the train to the bus for San Francisco, their luggage was waiting to be picked up at the San Francisco terminal.

As mentioned elsewhere in the book, the Santa Fe changed the final terminal for passenger trains to Richmond instead of Oakland during the late 1950s. The 1960 time table shows the *San Francisco Chief* departing Chicago at 3:15 p.m. with an arrival at Richmond at 1:30 p.m. on the second day. This was a 48 hour, 15 minute schedule for the 2529.3 mile route. Eastbound No. 2 departed Richmond at 11:59 a.m. with an arrival in Chicago at 2:00 p.m. the second day for basically a 48 hour, 1 minute train ride.

The *San Francisco Chief* continued to operate a variety of Pullman Sleeping Cars between Chicago and Richmond as well as Chicago to Tulsa and Lubbock. The train consist also included the Big Dome Lounge Car, Dining Car and 3 Chair Cars in each direction between Chicago and Richmond. An additional Chair Car operated between Chicago and Clovis.

The *San Francisco Chief* continued to have a number of additions and changes for the variety of train services and connections between Chicago and Richmond. For example, in 1964, the thru Chair Cars were replaced with Hi-level Chair Cars. The 1967 timetable lists four cars in each direction as part of the consist.

Refer to the Train Equipment Listings from the 1960 and 1967 Timetables in this chapter / section for a more detailed information of the variety of origins and destinations of the various Chair Car and Pullman Sleeper operations.

The last chapter of the *San Francisco Chief*, one could say, began in 1969. At that time, the Santa Fe had plans to reroute the *San Francisco Chief* into Los Angeles instead of its San Francisco service. Trains 1 and 2 at that time were coordinated with trains 23 and 24, which operated between Chicago and LA. 23 and 24 was the former *Grand Canyon*. The train was substantially shorter because of the loss of the mail contracts. The objective of the Santa Fe was to

The time is July, 1956 and the Hi-level *El Capitan* has just gone into service. Originally the train consisted of a Baggage Car, a Dormitory Baggage Car with a modified roof to match the Hi-level equipment, three Hi-level Chair Cars, Hi-level Dining Car, Hi-level Lounge and four more Hi-level Chair Cars. A truly beautiful train that provided the ultimate Chair Car Comfort. (Santa Fe Railway, Patrick C. Dorin Collection)

concentrate on the Chicago - LA passenger services with the route change of the *Chief*, discontinuing trains 23 and 24. The new schedule for 1970 would have been arranged to connect with Southern Pacific trains at Los Angeles for various central and northern California destinations. This plan did not go through.

This photo illustrates the type of consist of the Hi-level *El Capitan*, which w̶ normally powered by 4 F units, two or three head-end cars and how the Ch̶ Cars were distributed throughout the train. The Dining Car and Lounge C̶ were placed in the middle of the train for the convenience of passengers go̶ to and from the cars for meals, watching the scenery, making new frier̶ while traveling, and simply relaxing. No. 21 is shown here westbou̶ descending the slope of Glorietta Pass near Lamy, New Mexico. (Santa Railway, John Sward Collection)

One shred of history is still in operation as we roll into the 21st Century. The name "Chief" still exists on a passenger train, Amtrak's *Southwest Chief* which operates over the now Burlington Northern and Santa Fe between Chicago and Los Angeles. Thus one can still ride on Santa Fe trackage on a Chief, and on Superliner Cars whose concept was born with the Hi-Level Chair Cars Created by the Atchison, Topeka & Santa Fe.

The *El Capitan* in Action: The Hi-level All-Coach train is passing a freight train on Canyon Diablo Bridge (Arizona) demonstrating the use of Traffic Control Systems whereby both main tracks could be used for train operation in either direction. (Santa Fe Railway, John Sward Collection)

The 1969 Edition of the *San Francisco Chief* included the Big Dome Lounge Car and Dining Car along with the Hi-level Chair Cars. What is interesting is that the train also handled single level Chair Cars for Richmond and Los Angeles for the Summer Season. The LA Chair Car was handled on trains 23 and 24 between Barstow and LA. A similar arrangement was in place for a Chicago - Los Angeles Sleeping Car.

A Courier Nurse Service was still part of the *San Francisco Chief's* service agenda in 1969. There is no doubt about it. Despite the financial problems caused by the sharp declines in rail passenger travel in the late 1960s, which led to Amtrak, the Santa Fe still operated top quality trains. The *San Francisco Chief* ended its career in 1971 with the start up of Amtrak.

One Final Word About the Route of the Chiefs and the El Capitan.

It is 1964, and the *Super Chief* and the *El Capitan* had been combined dur̶ the off seasons. The train operated as train 17 and 18 between Chicago a̶ LA, and when it operated as separate trains, it was 1st and 2nd 17 and 18̶ the dispatcher's offices. What is interesting is that the trains retained their ide̶ tity complete with their individual dining and lounge car for the sleeper a̶ chair sections of the two trains in one. This is but one example of the mot̶ power required for the two trains in one. Six units are powering the westbou̶ No. 17 out of La Junta, Colorado. (William S. Kuba)

Although we are well into the Streamlined Era, Steam Power was still prominent on many of the primary Santa Fe trains in the mid-1940s and beyond. The 3777 is handling train 19, the Chief, out of Las Vegas, New Mexico with a rather interesting mix consist of streamlined and heavy weight equipment. Note the 60 foot Railway Post Office car between the two baggage cars. (Santa Fe Railway, Kansas State Historical Society Collection)

It is August, 1947, and No. 19, the *Chief*, is departing Chicago and passing Clark Street south of the Dearborn Station. The 4-6-4 Hudson, No. 3461, has the bell ringing and the train is moving for its trip to Los Angeles. (Wallace W. Abbey, TLC Collection)

The *Chief* also ran with the new diesel motive power as the train departs Fort Madison, Iowa for the remainder of its trip to Chicago just before Thanksgiving in 1938. (Joseph Sleger, Willam S. Kuba Collection)

Santa Fe's ad campaigns of the 1940s-60s featured one of three themes. The first and most prevalent connectedthe railway to the Navajo Indian Nation and its member since the line ranthrough their terriotoryin the Southwest. The second showcased the spectacular desert scenery encountered along the road, and the thirdwas as this one, which showed the superb accommodations available on Santa's Fe trains.

When the Electro-Motive F units arrived, steam power was pretty much gone. Here is an example of a diesel powered *Chief* rounding a curve in the lush farmlands near Glendora, California. (Santa Fe Railway, Patrick C. Dorin Collection)

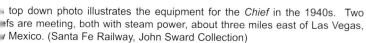

top down photo illustrates the equipment for the *Chief* in the 1940s. Two fs are meeting, both with steam power, about three miles east of Las Vegas, Mexico. (Santa Fe Railway, John Sward Collection)

Another steam powered *Chief* displays its Tail Sign in Cajon Pass as it crosses the Coast Range of Mountains in California. (Santa Fe Railway, Harry Stegmaier Collection)

The *Chief* was also powered by the Alco PAs as shown here with train No. 20 rolling by Pulaski Road dead on time into Chicago. (TLC Collection)

Still another example of Alco power on the head-end of the *Chief* with a mixed consist of heavyweight and streamlined equipment as it rolls by Arcadia, California. (TLC Collection)

Ultimately, the *Chief* became a Domeliner with a Big Dome Lounge car as part of the consist. The eastbound Chief, No. 20, is ascending the grade of Raton Pass shortly after leaving the city of Raton, New Mexico. Raton Pass is a short distance north of Raton. (Santa Fe Railway, John Sward Collection)

No. 20 has paused at San Bernardino, California as it begins its journey from Southern California to Chicago. The Observation Car brings up the rear proudly displaying the name "The Chief". (Santa Fe Railway, Harry Stegmaier Collection)

The *San Francisco Chief* equipment incorporating the Hi-level Chair Cars was displayed for the public at Fishermen's Wharf in San Francisco. It brought a new dimension to train service between Chicago and the Bay Area. Note the Big Dome Lounge Car ahead of the Hi-level Chair Cars. (Santa Fe Railway, Harry Stegmaier Collection)

The *San Francisco Chief* is nearing the Franklin Tunnel as it passes hillsides covered with blooming flowers of all types. The Big Dome is sixth car in the train behind the four Chair Cars and single baggage car - in the days prior to the Hi-level Chair Cars on the *San Francisco Chief*. (Santa Fe Railway, Patrick C. Dorin Collection)

The *San Francisco Chief* is crossing the Muir Trestle near Glen Frazer, California with its Hi-level Chair Cars and the Big Dome Lounge Car. (Santa Fe Railway, Harry Stegmaier Collection)

Right: The Santa Fe invested in General Electric U28CGs in 1966, number series 350 to 359. Three U28CGs, led by the 350, are powering an 18 car *Texas Chief* through the Arbuckle Mountains of Oklahoma. (Santa Fe Railway, Patrick C. Dorin Collection)

28

"Whe-e-e-ew
the New Super Chief!"

Just wait, cowboys, till you ride it!
The new Super Chief, all new from head-end to tail sign,
will embody up-to-the-minute rail travel features,
providing the utmost comfort in smooth-riding speed.
The schedule will be new, too!
The Super Chief will depart from Chicago and Los Angeles every day.
This fine all-first-class streamliner
will be one of a whole fleet of new Santa Fe trains soon to be announced.

SANTA FE SYSTEM LINES... Serving the West and Southwest
T. B. Gallaher, General Passenger Traffic Manager, Chicago 4

The *Texas Chief* was the way to go between Texas and Chicago. He[re] the eastbound train, No. 16, is rolling by Dalton Junction. The Juncti[on] was the meeting point from Fort Worth and Galveston and the new line [to] Dallas. (Santa Fe Railway, Kansas State Historical Society Collection[)]

The *San Francisco Chief*, train No. 1, is at the Joliet, Illinois depot on a very pleasant day in May, 1969. The Santa Fe was still providing the best of all possible passenger services. Amtrak was still two years away. (William S. Kuba)

something new to
remember
every magic mile

Maybe it's one of the many colorful sights you see in the Indian country along the Santa Fe.

Maybe it's the friendly train crew or some new feature of your Santa Fe train . . . an added comfort . . . or an extra service.

Whatever it may be, you'll find something new to remember every magic mile when you travel Santa Fe between Chicago and California. Five famous trains each day, each way. For reservations, just see your local ticket agent or travel agent.

YOU CAN HARDLY WAIT for mealtime . . . that wonderful Fred Harvey food is all you've heard about it.

Super Chief · Chief · El Capitan · Grand Canyon · California Ltd.
Texas Chief between Chicago-Texas • Kansas City Chief between Chicago-Kansas City

R. T. Anderson, General Passenger Traffic Manager, Santa Fe System Lines, Chicago 4, Illinois

These ads are typical of Santa Fe's treatment of the Navajo Indian theme in it advertising. Venders could usually be seen at major stations in Arizona and New Mexico selling turquoise Indian jewelry.

The Chief
is still the Chief

Now—only 39½ hours Chicago-Los Angeles...Only one night en route westbound...Extra fare dropped...Reserved seat chair cars...Same fine Pullman accommodations...Fred Harvey food—from full-course menus to low-cost budget meals.

Also . . . *Super Chief extra fare now only $7.50 on this all-private-room streamliner, Chicago-Los Angeles.*
El Capitan extra fare dropped on this only all-chair-car streamliner, Chicago-Los Angeles.

Santa Fe

America's New Railroad

There is no doubt about it, the Santa Fe *Chiefs* were the way to travel from Chicago to Kansas City, Texas and California and many points in between. Four of the passenger consists are lined-up here at the Chicago Yard with the Superb Observation Cars displaying the Train Names. (Santa Fe Railway, Harry Stegmaier Collection)

Here are two examples of Santa Fe box cars advertising the *Chiefs*, in this case the *San Francisco Chief* and the *Texas Chief*. (Bob's Photos)

Left column — Train 19

TRAIN 19 CHICAGO - LOS ANGELES
SUMMER 1966

LOADING NUMBER				
	1	60' RPO	Chicago	Kansas City
	1	Baggage-Mail (See Note 1)	"	Los Angeles
	1	Baggage-Dorm	"	"
08	1	CC Regular	"	"
07	1	CC Regular	"	"
06	1	CC Second Extra (5/27/66)	"	"
02	1	CC First Extra (4/25/66)	"	"
	1	LCDD	"	"
01	1	CC Regular	"	"
00	1	CC Regular	"	"
	1	Dome-Lounge	"	"
	1	Diner	"	"
96	1	2-4-4 (Diagram 235-D)	"	"
97	1	6-6-4 (Diagram 282-D)	"	"
98	1	10-6 (Diagram 216-D)	"	"
T-1	1	CC	"	Tulsa (For 211 at K.C.
D-2	1	CC	"	Dallas (For 11 at K.C.
D-3	1	CC	"	(For 11 at K.C.
	18	Cars Chicago-Kansas City		

AT KANSAS CITY SWITCH OUT

T-1	1	60' RPO	Chicago	Kansas City
D-2	1	CC	"	Tulsa
D-3	1	CC	"	Dallas
	1	CC	"	

AT KANSAS CITY SWITCH IN

	1	SM	Kansas City	Los Angeles
	1	60' RPO	" "	La Junta
	1	EM (On rear)	" "	Dodge City
	17	Cars Kansas City-Dodge City		

AT DODGE CITY SWITCH OUT

| | 1 | EM (On rear) | Kansas City | Dodge City |
| | 16 | Cars Dodge City-La Junta | | |

AT LA JUNTA SWITCH OUT

| | 1 | 60' RPO | Kansas City | La Junta |
| | 15 | Cars La Junta-Los Angeles | | |

NOTE 1: On half of space behind rear left side doorway loaded with checked baggage May 25-Sept. 10.

This consist illustrates the westbound *Chief*, train No. 19, from Chicago to Los Angeles during the Summer of 1966. Note the various origins and destinations and the switching instructions at Kansas City, Dodge City and La Junta. (Santa Fe Passenger Consist, 1966)

Right column — Trains 10, 11, 111

TRAIN 10
KANSAS CITY - CHICAGO

	1	Baggage-Express	Houston - Chicago, Daily (Off Train 6)
	1	Baggage-Mail (TBMar)	Kansas City - Chicago, Daily
	1	Storage Mail	Kansas City - Chicago (Sealed) Extra
	1	Express	" " - " "
	3	Chairs	" " - " "
	1	Lounge	" " - " "
4511	1	10-6	" " - " "
4520	1	6-6-4	" " - " "
4509	1	10-5	" " - " "
4516	1	24-Duplex	" " - " "
4503	1	10-3-2	Tulsa - Chicago (Off 47 Kansas City)
4505	1	6-6-4	Topeka - Chicago (Off Train 6 Kansas City)

14 cars Kansas City to Chicago

TRAIN 11
KANSAS CITY - OKLAHOMA CITY

	1	Stge Mail (LIFE)(LW)	Chicago - Houston, Tues-Wed. (Off Train 19)
	1	Express (LIFE)(LW)	Chicago - Dallas, Tuesday (Off Train 19)
	1	Stge Mail (LW)	Kansas City - Fort Worth, Daily
	1	Express-Mail (LW)	" " - Oklahoma City, Daily
	1	Bage-Dorm. (LW)	" " - " "
4018	1	8-2-2	" " - Dallas (For 111 Oklahoma City)
	1	Dome	" " - Oklahoma City
	2	Chairs	" " - " "
	1	LCD	" " - " "
	1	Chair	" " - Dallas (For 111 Oklahoma City)

9 cars Kansas City to Oklahoma City (10 cars Wed., 11 cars Tues.

TRAIN 111
OKLAHOMA CITY - FORT WORTH

	1	Stge Mail (LIFE)(LW)	Chicago - Houston, Wed-Thurs. (For Train 15 Ft.Wor
	1	Express (LIFE)(LW)	Chicago - Dallas, Wednesday
	1	Storage Mail (LW)	Kansas City - Fort Worth, Daily
	1	Storage Mail	Oklahoma City - Dallas, Daily
	1	30-40' Combn.	" " - Fort Worth, Daily
	1	Chair	" " - Dallas
	1	Chair	Chicago - Dallas
4018	1	8-2-2	Kansas City - Dallas

6 cars Oklahoma City to Fort Worth (8 cars Wed., 7 cars Thurs.)

The *Kansas City Chief* No. 10 continued to run as a separate train overnight from Kansas City to Chicago in 1957. Later it was combined with the eastbound *Chief* but continued as a westbound overnight train service into the 1960s. (Santa Fe Passenger Consist, 1957)

Bottom left — Train 9

TRAIN 9, CHICAGO TO KANSAS CITY

	1	P.Box Exp.	Chicago - Dallas, Daily (For MK&T)
	1	Express	Chicago-Wichita-Okla.City, Ex Sun.-Mon)For
	1	Stge Mail	Chicago-Wichita-Okla.City, Ex Sun-Mon) 3
	1	Exp-Mail	Chicago-Wichita-Okla.City, Sun-Mon) Kans.
	1	Baggage (TBM)	Chicago-Los Angeles, Daily) City
	1	Stge Mail (Local)	Chicago-Kansas City, Daily
		(Extra sealed carloads mail & express for Kansas City & West)	
	1	Express	Philadelphia - Kansas City, Ex Mon-Tue-Wed
	1/3	Stge Mail	Hoboken-Kans City--As rec'd from E-L RR.
	2	CC	Chicago - Kansas City
	1	Dome-Lounge	" " "
93	1	10-6	" " "

NOTE: During summer months the LCD for #11 will deadhead on #9, Chicago-Kansas City.

Here is a snap shot of the westbound *Kansas City Chief*, No. 9 in 1966. The head-end business has been expanded for this train consist, but there has been a reduction in the number of passenger carrying cars. Note the through head-end cars from Erie-Lackawanna en route to Kansas City. (Santa Fe Passenger Consist, 1966)

Page 10

The *Texas Chief* was truly a great way to travel between Chicago and Texas. In addition to at least five sleeping cars, the train also ran with six chair cars. Note the switching moves at Kansas City, Wichita and Fort Worth. (Santa Fe Passenger Consist, 1959)

Train 15 Chicago to Houston

	1	60-ft RPO	Chicago	Kansas City (Exc. Sun)
	1	BME	"	Houston
	1	30-40 Combn.	"	"
	4	CC	"	"
	2	CC	"	Dallas
	1	Diner	"	Houston
	1	Lounge	"	"
158	1	10-6	"	"
156	1	2-4-4	"	Fort Worth
154	1	10-6	"	Dallas
151	1	10-3-2	"	Wichita

15 cars Chicago-Kansas City (Mon-Sat)
14 cars Chicago-Kansas City (Sun   )

AT KANSAS CITY TAKE OFF

	1	60 ft. RPO	Chicago	Kansas City

ADD

	1	SM	Kansas City	Fort Worth

15 cars Kansas City-Wichita

AT WICHITA TAKE OFF

151	1	10-3-2	Chicago	Wichita

14 cars Wichita-Gainesville

The *San Francisco Chief* had several switching maneuvers en route from Chicago to Los Angeles. This consist shows the operating line up for train No. 1 in 1957. (Santa Fe Passenger Consist, 1957)

(Page 1)

PULLMAN
LINE

TRAIN 1
CHICAGO - KANSAS CITY

	1	Bage-Exp-Mail	Chicago	- Oakland
	1	Chair	"	- Clovis
	5	Chairs	"	- Oakland
	1	LCD	"	- "
	1	Dome	"	- "
	1	Diner	"	- "
4025	1	4-1-Lounge	"	- "
4024	1	10-3-2	"	- "
4023	1	6-6-4	"	- Lubbock (For 93 Amarillo)
4503	1	10-3-2	"	- Tulsa (For 47 Kansas City)

14 cars Chicago to Kansas City.

TRAIN 1
KANSAS CITY - OAKLAND

	1	Bage-Exp-Mail	Chicago	- Oakland
	1 or 2	Storage Mail	Kansas City	- Oakland
	1	Chair	Chicago	- Clovis
	5	Chairs	"	- Oakland
	1	Chair	Houston	- "
	1	LCD	Chicago	- "
	1	Dome	"	- "
	1	Diner	"	- "
4025	1	4-1-Lounge	"	- "
4024	1	10-3-2	"	- "
4518	1	10-6	Kansas City	- Oakland
4506	1	8-2-2	Houston	- Oakland (Off 76 Clovis)
4023	1	6-6-4	Chicago	- Lubbock (For 93 Amarillo)

15 or 16 cars Kansas City to Amarillo
14 or 15 "   Amarillo to Clovis
15 or 16 "   Clovis to Oakland

```
                 Consolidated Train 17 Sept 15, 1959
Loading
Number                          Chicago - Los Angeles

      1  SM                Chicago - Kans City Daily Exc Sun-Mon
      1  SM                   "        Los Angs  Daily
      1  Bage-Dorm            "          "   "     "
906   1  Hi-Level CC Stepdown "          "   "     "
904   1  Hi-Level CC          "          "   "   Mon and Thu only
      1  Hi-Level Diner       "          "   "   Daily
      1  Hi-Level Lounge      "          "   "     "
903   1  Hi-Level CC          "          "   "     "
900   1  Hi-Level CC Stepdown "          "   "     "
176   1  10-6                 "          "   "     "
174   1  4-4-2                "          "   "     "
      1  Dome-Lounge          "          "   "     "
      1  Diner                "          "   "     "
172   1  4-4-2                "          "   "     "
171   1  10-6                 "          "   "     "
     15  cars Chicago - Kansas City Thursday
     14  cars Chicago - Kansas City Mon-Tue-Wed-Fri and Sat
     13  cars Chicago - Kansas City Sunday

         At Kansas City switch out SM Chicago-Kansas City, and
         switch in its place:

         SM Kans City-LA, Wed-Thu-Sat; or SM(Dayton)KC-LA Sun,
170      switch 10-6 sleeper on rear daily.

     15  cars Kansas City-La Junta, Tue-Wed-Thu-Fri-Sat-Sun
     14  cars Kansas City-La Junta, Monday

         At La Junta switch 60-ft RPO in ahead of SM Chicago-
         Los Angeles daily.

     16  cars La Junta-Los Angeles, Tue-Wed-Thu-Fri-Sat-Sun
     15  cars La Junta-Los Angeles, Monday

         From Kansas City on Friday half of dormitory-baggage
         car reserved for mail.
```

One example of a passenger consist make-up of the combined *Super Chief* and *El Capitan*, train No. 17, in 1959. (Santa Fe Passenger Consist, 1959)

It is the summer of 1966, and the *El Capitan* and the *Super Chief* ran separately, or as 1st and 2nd 17 and 18 between Chicago and Los Angeles. This consist illustrates 2nd No. 18, the *Super Chief* with its mixed consist of Chair Cars and Sleeping Cars. Note that there are separate lounge and dining facilities for both parts of the 15 car train. (Santa Fe Consist, 1966)

```
                                                        PAGE 18

          SUPER CHIEF TRAIN 18 LOS ANGELES-CHICAGO 2ND SECTION
                              SUMMER

   LOADING        DAILY
   NUMBER         CARS

                    1    Baggage TBM   Los Angeles         Chicago
   1834             1    CC (1)          "       "           "
   1833             1    CC              "       "           "
   1832             1    CC              "       "           "
   1831             1    CC              "       "           "
   1830             1    CC              "       "           "
                    1    Lounge-Dorm (2) "      "            "
                    1    LCD (3)         "       "           "
   186              1    10-6            "       "           "
   184              1    11-Bedroom      "       "           "
                    1    Dome-Lounge     "       "           "
                    1    Diner           "       "           "
   182              1    11-Bedroom      "       "           "
   181              1    11-Bdrm or 4-4-2(4) "   "           "
   180              1    10-6            "       "       Kansas City
                   15 Cars Los Angeles-Kansas City

                   AT KANSAS CITY SWITCH OUT
   180              1    10-6        Los Angeles       Kansas City
                   14 Cars Kansas City-Chicago

   NOTE: (1)     News Agent Seats 2-4-6-8
         (2)     Dorm to Head-End
         (3)     Kitchen to Rear
         (4)     11-Bedroom Monday, Wednesday and Saturday
```

Chapter 3 - A FLEET OF NAME TRAINS

El Capitan

The Santa Fe was famous for its streamliner fleet of *Chiefs*, and also for a group of still more passenger services that played a crucial role in the entire service picture. Many of these trains from the 1950s on were equipped with streamlined cars, and were delightful to ride, watch and to enjoy railroading. It also added even more inspiration for the Art of Model Railroading, which carries on even more so as we move into the 21st Century. Santa Fe passenger service was the "Way to Go".

This chapter takes a look at the group of limited and other name trains in operation the last two decades before Amtrak. What were the names of the many trains in operation during the early 1950s, 60s, and what the group had dwindled down to in the late 1960s with the nationwide loss of passenger patronage and service. It goes without saying that this a brief overview of the various train services in this category. Santa Fe passenger service history has one of the most unique system operations to be found anywhere in the world. Yes, it was that good and even more. Finally it cannot be over emphasized on how the Santa Fe continued to provide the highest qualities of service right to the beginning of Amtrak.

THE GRAND CANYON

The *Grand Canyon* was a transcontinental train between Chicago and Los Angeles with through cars for San Francisco. The train was designated as a Fast Daily Train between Chicago and California with 47 1/2 hours to Los Angeles, and 54 3/4 hours to San Francisco in 1953. The train provided both Pullman Sleeping and Chair Car Services. The train operated as train 23 and 24 between Chicago and LA, as its Southern Section, and as 123 and 124 for its Northern Section. The trains were combined between Chicago and Kansas City, and the two split or combined westbound or eastbound respectively. The train crew also included a Courier-Nurse.

The Southern Section of the *Grand Canyon*, trains 23 and 24 operated via Clovis and Belen, while the Northern Section, trains 123 and 124, operated via La Junta and Albuquerque. The passenger equipment on the two trains were for the most part lightweight streamlined cars by the early 1950s.

As the 1950s came to a close and time moved into 1960, trains 23 and 24 had been discontinued. The *Grand Canyon* continued to operate as trains 123 and 124 between Chicago and Los Angeles. Numbers 123 and 124 operated via La Junta. The westbound departed Chicago at 11:00 a.m. with an arrival at Los Angeles at 12:10 p.m. for a 51 hour, 10 minute run. Eastbound 124 departed Los Angeles at 1:15 p.m. with a Chicago arrival time of 5:30 p.m. for a 50 hour, 15 minute run in 1960.

The train continued to provided both Pullman and Chair car service, but through cars were no longer operated to San Francisco. The San Francisco service had been replaced with the new and faster *San Francisco Chief*. The consist of the train included the Dormitory Lounge Car and Dining Car as well as two Pullmans between Chicago and Los Angeles, one Pullman between Kansas City and LA, and one Pullman between Dallas and Los Angeles. The Dallas sleeper was a bit complicated with a series of trains between Dallas and Barstow westbound, and from Winslow to Dallas eastbound.

Looking ahead five plus years to 1966, the *Grand Canyon* again operated with train numbers 23 and 24. It was part of the fleet of five trains each way daily between Chicago and California. Westbound 23 made the trip in 51 hours, 10 minutes while eastbound 24 did the run in 48 hours. Sleeping Cars and Chair Cars were part of the consist for this relaxing train ride that provided a substantial amount of intermediate services along the main between Chicago and Los Angeles.

Moving to 1969, the *Grand Canyon* was a relatively short train compared to its past years of superb service. First of all, trains 23 and 24 had basically lost the name *Grand Canyon*. No. 23 departed Chicago at 9:00 a.m. with a Los Angeles arrival 6:00 a.m. for a total travel time of 47 hours. Eastbound 24 departed LA at 9:00 p.m. with an arrival in Chicago at 9:00 p.m., the second evening for a running time of 46 hours. The only through equipment on 23 and 24 between Chicago and LA were Chair Cars. The Lunch Counter Dining Car operated between Chicago and Barstow. The train handled an additional Chair Car between Barstow and Los Angeles during the summer season, which operated on the *San Francisco Chief* between Chicago and Barstow. One Sleeping Car for Chicago - LA service was also handled on the *San Francisco Chief* between Chicago and Barstow.

Things had change rather dramatically since the early 1950s when the *Grand Canyon* operated as two sections between Kansas City and Los Angeles. The Santa Fe had wanted to discontinue 23 and 24 and replace it with the *San Francisco Chief* between Chicago and LA, but such was not to be. By 1970, it would not be long until the Amtrak Chapter on Passenger Services began, and trains 23 and 24 would be no longer operating on the main line.

No. 1 San Francisco Chief Daily Example	No. 9-5 The Ranger Daily Example	No. 15 Texas Chief Daily Example	No. 19-11-111 TheKansasCityan Daily Example	Miles	**Table D** Chicago, Kansas, Oklahoma and Texas	No. 16 Texas Chief Daily Example	No. 6-20 The Ranger Daily Example	No. 112-12 Chicago Express Daily Example	No. 20 The Chief Daily Example
3.15PM Sun.	10.00PM Sun.	6.00PM Sun.	9.10AM Sun.	0	Lv....Chicago (C.S.T.)....Ar	9.00AM Mon.	7.15PM Tues.	8.00PM Mon.	7.15PM Tues.
10.30PM "	7.00AM Mon.	1.30AM Mon.	4.35PM "	451	Ar....Kansas City....Lv	1.10AM "	11.00PM "	12.25PM "	11.00PM " Mon.
No. 47			**No. 211**					**No. 212**	**No. 48**
11.59PM Sun.			5.00PM Sun.	451	Lv....Kansas City....Ar	12.50AM Mon.		12.10PM Mon.	10.00PM Mon.
12.40AM Mon.			5.25PM "	477	"....Olathe.... "			11.33AM "	9.20PM "
1.30AM "			6.00PM "	509	"....Ottawa.... "			11.00AM "	8.40PM "
2.10AM "			6.25PM "	534	"....Garnett.... "			10.30AM "	8.00PM "
2.45AM "			7.05PM "	560	"....Iola.... "			10.05AM "	7.25PM "
3.30AM "			7.25PM "	577	"....Chanute.... "			9.50AM "	7.03PM "
4.10AM "			7.55PM "	607	"....Cherryvale.... "			9.12AM "	6.20PM "
4.35AM "			8.10PM "	616	Ar....Independence....Lv			9.02AM "	6.08PM "
4.35AM "			8.10PM "	639	Lv....Independence....Ar			9.00AM "	6.08PM "
5.10AM "			8.34PM "	639	"....Caney....Lv			8.31AM "	5.40PM "
5.45AM "			8.57PM "	657	"....Bartlesville....Lv			8.10AM "	5.15PM "
7.00AM "			10.00PM "	707	"....Tulsa (C.S.T.)....Lv			7.15AM "	4.10PM "
	No. 5	**No. 15**	**No.11-111**			**No. 16**	**No. 6**	**No.112-12**	
	8.30AM Mon.	1.50AM Mon.	5.05PM Sun.	451	Lv....Kansas City....Ar	12.50AM Mon.	9.15PM Mon.	12.05PM Mon.	
	9.45AM "	3.45AM "	6.15PM "	517	"....Topeka.... "	11.00PM "	7.40PM "	10.50AM "	
	11.25AM "	5.00AM "	7.20PM "	578	"....Emporia.... "	9.50PM Sun.	6.10PM "	9.45AM "	
	12.55PM "	5.35AM "	7.30PM "	636	"....Newton.... "	9.15PM "	4.35PM "	8.35AM "	
	1.35PM "	6.40AM "	9.05PM "	663	Ar....Wichita....Lv	8.12PM "	3.50PM "	8.00AM "	
	3.15PM "	7.08AM "	10.10PM "	715	"....Arkansas City.... "	7.38PM "	2.30PM "	7.05AM "	
	3.57PM "	8.07AM "	10.40PM "	740	"....Ponca City.... "	6.35PM "	1.43PM "	6.33AM "	
	5.22PM "	8.55AM "	11.45PM "	804	"....Guthrie.... "	6.00PM "	12.25PM "	5.33AM "	
	6.15PM "	9.40AM "	12.30AM Mon.	835	"....Oklahoma City.... "	5.13PM "	11.40AM "	5.00AM "	
	7.25PM "	11.52AM "	2.00AM "	868	"....Purcell.... "		10.35AM "	3.20AM "	
	9.46PM "		5.00AM "	975	Ar....Gainesville....Lv		8.05AM "	12.05AM "	
	No. 115					**No. 116**			
	12.33PM Mon.			1021	Ar....Denton....Lv	2.20PM Sun.			
	1.20PM "			1062	"...White Rock (No. Dallas)...	1.35PM "			
	1.55PM "			1075	Ar....Dallas....Lv	1.10PM "			
	9.46PM Mon.	11.52AM Mon.	5.00AM Mon.	975	Lv....Gainesville....Ar	3.03PM Sun.	8.05AM Mon.	12.05AM Mon.	
	10.55PM "	12.55PM "	6.30AM "	1040	Ar....Ft. Worth....Lv	2.00PM "	7.00AM "	10.20PM "	
		7.00AM Mon.	7.45AM Mon.	1040	Lv....Ft. Worth....Ar		▲16.25AM Mon.		
			7.45AM "	1071	Ar....Dallas (Railway Station)....Lv		▲15.13AM "		
					Ar....Dallas (Bus Station)....Lv		▲15.10AM "		
	▲12.10AM Tues.	▲11.10AM Mon.	8.15PM Mon.	0	Lv Dallas (Bus Station)....Ar	▲3.25PM Sun.	7.45AM "	9.09PM Sun.	
	▲1.20AM "	▲11.13AM "	9.00AM "		Lv Dallas (Railway Station)....Ar		7.45AM "	8.15PM "	
	▲1.25AM "	▲12.25PM "		31	Lv....Ft. Worth....Lv	▲2.10PM "	7.00AM "		
	8.15PM Mon.		9.20PM Mon.	0	Lv....Ft. Worth....Ar	9.20PM Mon.	5.45AM Mon.		
	9.00PM "		1.25AM Tue.	142	Ar....Brownwood....Lv	1.00AM "			
			6.10AM "	232	Ar....San Angelo....Lv	8.50PM Sun.			
	11.20PM Mon.	1.05PM Mon.		1040	Lv....Ft. Worth....Ar	1.45PM Sun.	6.05AM Mon.		
	2.30AM Tues.	3.27PM "		1168	"....Temple.... "	11.31AM "	2.45AM "		
	8.00AM "	7.00PM "		1357	"....Houston.... "	8.10AM "	9.25PM "		
		8.15PM "		1410	Ar....Galveston (C.S.T.)....Lv	6.50AM "			

TEXAS CHIEF
Trains 15 and 16

Streamliner Service, Pullman and Chair Cars

Sleeping Car ..Chicago and Ft. Worth—2 D. R., 4 Comps., 4 D. B. R. Car 156 (southbound); Car 166 (northbound). Chicago and Houston—10 Roomettes, 6 D. B. R. Car 155 (southbound); Car 168 (northbound). Chicago and Wichita—10 Roomettes, 3 D. B. R., 2 Comps. (May be occupied until 8:00 a.m. at Wichita.) Car 151 (southbound); car 161 (northbound).
Lounge Car Service all the way.
Dining Car....Chicago and Houston. (Fred Harvey Service). Coffee and sandwiches available between Gainesville and Dallas.
Chair Car.....Chicago and Houston. Houston and Galveston.
Sleeping Car ..Chicago and Dallas—10 Roomettes, 6 D. B. R. Car 154 (southbound); Car 164 (northbound).
Chair Car.....Chicago and Dallas.

THE TULSAN
Trains 211 and 212

Chair Car.............Chicago and Kansas City.
Chair Car.............Chicago and Tulsa.
Dining Car............Chicago and Kansas City. (Fred Harvey Service);
Snack Car.............Kansas City and Tulsa.
Lounge Car............Chicago and Kansas City.

THE KANSAS CITYAN—THE CHICAGOAN
Trains 19-11-111 and 112-12

Streamliner Service, Pullman and Chair Cars.

Lounge Car.............Chicago and Oklahoma City.
Chair Cars.............Chicago and Oklahoma City. Chicago and Dallas. Kansas City and Oklahoma City.
Lunch Counter-Dining Car..Chicago and Oklahoma City. Serving all meals. (Fred Harvey Service).

THE RANGER
Trains 9-5 and 6-20

Pullman and Chair Car Service

Lounge Car.............Chicago and Kansas City.
Sleeping Car...........Chicago and Topeka—6 Roomette, 6 Sec., 4 Double Bedrooms Car 56 (westbound); Car 66 (eastbound).
Dining Car.............Kansas City to Chicago. (Fred Harvey Service).
Coffee Cart Service....Kansas City and Ft. Worth (Sandwiches, coffee, milk and other refreshments. Fred Harvey Service).
Chair Car.............Chicago and Kansas City. Kansas City and Houston.

THE OIL FLYER
Trains 47 and 48.

Lounge Car.......Chicago and Kansas City. (On Train 1 and 20).
Sleeping Car......Chicago and Tulsa—10 Roomette, 3 D. B. R., 2 Comps. (On train 1 and 20 between Chicago and Kansas City. Car 471 (southbound); Car 481 (northbound). Pullman may be occupied at Tulsa until 8.00 a.m.
Dining Car........Chicago and Kansas City. (Fred Harvey Service).
Chair Car.........Chicago and Kansas City. Kansas City and Tulsa.
Snack Car........Kansas City and Tulsa.

Explanatory Notes and Reference Marks: Sec.—Section; D. R.—Drawing room; Comps—Compartment; D. B. R.—Double Bedroom. † Daily except Sunday. ▲ Via Texas Motor Coaches.

The Santa Fe operated a fleet of name trains as well as the Fleet of Chiefs. Table D from the Spring, 1960 timetable illustrated the schedules of the Texas Chief along with five other trains.

Drawing Room cars. The train also handled a fair amount of head-end traffic of mail and express.

The *California Limited* was no longer part of the Santa Fe fleet by 1957. With the *San Francisco Chief*, and the enhancement of the other Streamliner services, trains 3 and 4 melded into the operations and services of the extraordinary Santa Fe fleet.

THE KANSAS CITYAN AND CHICAGOAN

The *Kansas Cityan*, train 11, was a day time train service from Chicago to Kansas City, while its eastbound counterpart train 12, the *Chicagoan*, provided day time service to Chicago. The train was designated a Lightweight Streamlined train with Chair Cars, Chair Lounge Car, Dining Car and a Parlor Observation car. During the early 1950s, trains 11 and 12 operated between Chicago and Kansas City. This would change a bit by the mid-1950s. Numbers 11 and 12 no longer operated between Chicago and Kansas City as such in 1957.

Number 11 had been combined with train 19, the *Chief* between Chicago and Kansas City. From there No. 11 operated from Kansas City to Oklahoma City, while No. 111 continued to Oklahoma City to Dallas. Eastbound, No. 112 operated from Dallas to Oklahoma City, and from there No. 12 continued the remainder of the distance to Chicago. The trains were still designated as the *Kansas Cityan* and the *Chicagoan* with the day time schedules between Chicago and Kansas City. In addition to the Lunch Counter Dining Car between Chicago and Oklahoma City, the train also provided Sleeping Car service between Dallas and Kansas City. Trains 19-11-111 to Kansas City and to Chicago as trains 112-12 were still designated as the *Kansas Cityan* and the *Chicagoan* in 1960.

The train continued to hold its own through 1966 with the same names, and the train numbers 19-11 and 12. The train was designated a streamlined train during the mid-1960s. The Pullman Sleeping car between Kansas City and Dallas was a 6 Section, 6 Roomette and 4 Double Bedroom Car. A Lunch Counter - Dining Car was part of the consist between Chicago and Wichita according to a 1966

THE CALIFORNIA LIMITED

The *California Limited* was still another transcontinental passenger train operating between Chicago and Los Angeles as trains 3 and 4 during the early 1950s. The train provided Chair Car Service between Chicago and LA as well as to Oakland. Additional Chair Car service operated between Phoenix and Los Angeles. Sleeping car service was also available between Chicago and LA, Chicago and Albuquerque, Chicago and Oakland, and Chicago and Galveston. A through Lounge Car operated on 3 and 4 between Chicago and LA, while the Dining Car was primarily a Chicago La Junta operation at that time.

No. 3 departed Chicago at 8:45 p.m. and arrived in LA at 6:30 a.m. the third morning. Eastbound No. 4 departed LA at 6:15 p.m. and arrived in Chicago at 8:30 a.m. the third morning. In 1953, the Sleeping Cars were still heavy weight cars, such as the 8 Section, 2 Compartment and 1

Dallas, Ft. Worth, Brownwood and San Angelo Via Brownwood				
WEST—Read down			EAST—Read up	
No. 112-77 The Angelo Daily Example	Mls.	Table **M**	No. 78-111 The Angelo Daily Example	
8.15PM Sun.	0	Lv......Dallas (C.S.T.)...Ar	7.45AM Mon.	
9.00PM "	31	Ar......Ft. Worth......Lv	7.00AM "	
9.20PM Sun.	31	Lv......Ft. Worth......Ar	5.45AM Mon.	
f10.04PM "	56	"......Cresson......Lv	5.01AM "	
11.19PM "	107	"......Stephenville....."	3.20AM "	
11.48PM "	121	"......Dublin......"	2.48AM "	
1.25AM Mon.	173	Ar....Brownwood....Lv	1.00AM "	
2.30AM "	173	Lv....Brownwood....Ar	12.05AM "	
4.47AM "	227	Ar......Ballinger......Lv	10.00PM Sun.	
6.10AM "	263	"....San Angelo (C.S.T.)...."	8.50PM "	

THE ANGELO
Equipment

Trains 111 and 112 between Dallas and Fort Worth; Trains 77 and 78 Fort Worth and San Angelo.

Chair Car....Dallas—Ft. Worth and San Angelo.

Dallas, Ft. Worth and Clovis Via Brownwood					
WEST—Read down				EAST—Read up	
No. 112-77- 75 The California Special Daily Example	Mls.	Table **N**		No. 76-78- 111 The Texan Daily Example	
8.15PM Sun.	0	Lv.....Dallas (C.S.T.)....Ar		7.45AM Mon.	
9.00PM "	31	Ar......Ft. Worth......Lv		7.00AM "	
9.20PM "	31	Lv......Ft. Worth......Ar		5.45AM "	
11.48PM "	121	"......Dublin......"		2.48AM "	
1.25AM Mon.	170	Lv....Brownwood....Ar		1.00AM "	
2.00AM "	170	Ar....Brownwood....Lv		12.25AM "	
4.25AM "	284	Lv....Sweetwater....."		9.50PM Sun.	
6.55AM "	390	Lv......Slaton......"		7.40PM "	
7.30AM "	406	"......Lubbock......"		7.15PM "	
10.30AM "	494	Ar......Clovis (C.S.T.)....Lv		4.26PM "	

Equipment

Trains 112-77 and 78-111 between Dallas and Brownwood; Trains 75 and 76 Brownwood and Clovis.

Sleeping Car...Dallas and Clovis— 6 Roomette, 6 Sec., 4 D.B.R.
Chair Car......Dallas and Clovis.
Dining Car....Brownwood and Clovis.

Houston and San Angelo				
WEST—Read down			EAST—Read up	
No. 66-75-77 California Special The Angelo Daily Example	Mls.	Table **O**	No. 78-76-65 The Angelo- California Special Daily Example	
6.45PM Sun.	0	Lv.....Houston (C.S.T.)....Ar	8.15AM Mon.	
1.35AM Mon.	191	Ar......Temple......Lv	4.00AM "	
2.55AM "	334	"......Brownwood....."	12.45AM "	
3.21AM "	346	"......Bangs......"	11.38PM Sun.	
3.52AM "	361	"......Santa Anna....."	11.18PM "	
4.15AM "	371	"......Valera......"	10.49PM "	
4.47AM "	387	"......Taipa......"	10.33PM "	
5.07AM "	395	"......Ballinger......"	10.00PM "	
5.25AM "	404	"......Rowena......"	9.43PM "	
6.10AM "	423	Ar......San Angelo......Lv	8.50PM "	

Equipment

Trains 66 and 65 between Houston and Temple; Trains 75 and 76 between Temple and Brownwood; Trains 77 and 78 between Brownwood and San Angelo.

Chair Car....Houston and San Angelo. (with change)

Secondary trains included both names, such as the Angelo as well as trains without names such as illustrated in Tables M, N and O. (Spring, 1960 Time Table)

time table. By the end of the 1960s, the *Kansas Cityan* and the *Chicagoan* had been melded into still other train services between Chicago, Kansas City and Oklahoma and Texas points.

THE TULSAN

The *Tulsan* was a Lightweight Streamlined train, operating as 211 and 212 between Kansas City and Tulsa. The train provided service between Chicago and Tulsa and was combined with the Kansas Cityan from Chicago to Kansas City, and the *Chicagoan* from Kansas City to Chicago. The train provided through Chair Cars between Chicago and Tulsa as well as Cafe Lounge Car between Kansas City and Tulsa in 1953.

By 1957, the westbound *Tulsan* had been combined with the *Chief* between Chicago and Kansas City. The eastbound run continued with the Chicagoan. A Snack Car operated between Kansas City and Tulsa. This type of schedule held together through the 1960s. By 1969, the Tulsan, trains 211 and 212 between Kansas City and Tulsa were slated for abandonment. Passengers changed trains at Kansas City in both directions between Chicago and Tulsa. The Snack Car had been replaced with a Coffee-Sandwich Cart Service between Kansas City and Tulsa.

THE OIL FLYER

The companion train to the *Tulsan* was the *Oil Flyer*. The train provided Pullman Sleeping Car service between Chicago and Tulsa. The train operated as Numbers 47 and 48 between Kansas City and Tulsa in 1953. At that time, the Flyer was combined with the *Kansas City Chief* to Chicago, and the *Texas Chief* from Chicago to KC.

The train included a Dining Car between KC and Tulsa in 1953, but by 1957, trains 47 and 48 included only a Snack Car. The only through car was the 10 Roomette, 2 Compartment, 3 Double Bedroom Pullman Sleeper. Chair

Car passengers changed trains in Kansas City. This was also true in the early 1950s for Chair Car passengers. This operation for the *Oil Flyer* remained stable through the early 1960s.

Upon arrival of the mid-1960s, the *Oil Flyer* no longer provided Pullman Sleeping Car Service. Chair Car passengers changed trains at KC from the *San Francisco Chief* for Tulsa, and eastbound passengers changed at KC to the *Chicagoan*, train 12. Meal service was provided by a Coffee-Sandwich Cart between Tulsa and Independence. This period of time was part of the final chapter of the *Oil Flyer*.

THE EL PASOAN

The 1957 schedules simply indicated that the *El Pasoan*, trains 13 and 14, operated between Albuquerque and El Paso. No. 13 departed Albuquerque at 6:00 p.m. with an arrival at El Paso at 11:40 p.m. No. 14 departed El Paso at 8:00 a.m. and arrived at Albuquerque at 1:45 p.m. The run between the two terminals was 253 miles.

The same basic schedule existed in 1960. Trains 13 and 14 provided Chair Car Service only but continued to carry the name *El Pasoan*. In 1966, the train was designated a Streamliner and continued to operate southbound in the evening, and northbound in the morning. Trains 13 and 14 connected with the *Super Chief / El Capitan* at Albuquerque for El Paso passengers in both directions. The railroad now also provided a bus connection from Albuquerque to El Paso for connections with the *Chief* for El Paso, and with the *Grand Canyon* for eastern destinations. The end of the 1960s saw only bus connections for El Paso.

THE CALIFORNIA SPECIAL AND THE TEXAN

The *California Special* was a westbound train operation providing a combination of several trains with schedules between New Orleans and Los Angeles. The *Texan* provided the eastbound combination of trains between Los Angeles and New Orleans in 1953. The service included a through Pullman Sleeping Car operation in both directions between Oakland and New Orleans.

Looking forward to 1957, the *California Special* was now a designated train in both directions. However, there was no longer a New Orleans - Los Angeles - Oakland operation. The service had been trimmed a bit to be a Houston - LA - Oakland service with a combination of sev-

Albuquerque, Belen and El Paso

SOUTH—Read down   **NORTH—Read up**

No. 13 The El Pasoan Daily Example		Miles	Table F		No. 14 The El Pasoan Daily Example	
			Mountain Standard Time			
6.00PM	Sunday	0	Lv.............Albuquerque...........Ar		12.45PM	Sunday
f 6.15PM	"	13	"..............Isleta.............Lv		f12.21PM	"
6.22PM	"	20	"..............Los Lunas..........."		12.12PM	"
6.40PM	"	30	"..............Belen.............."		11.59AM	"
f 7.11PM	"	61	"..............San Acacia........."		f11.12AM	"
7.35PM	"	75	"..............Socorro..........."		10.55AM	"
f 7.46PM	"	86	"..............San Antonio........"		f10.38AM	"
f 8.52PM	"	141	"..............Engle............."		9.31AM	"
9.35PM	"	177	Ar.............Rincon............Lv		8.45AM	"
9.40PM	"	177	Lv.............Rincon............Ar		8.45AM	"
10.35PM	"	210	"..............Las Cruces........."		7.57AM	"
f10.38PM	"	213	"..............Mesilla Park......."		f 7.47AM	"
11.03PM	"	234	"..............Anthony..........."		7.24AM	"
f11.12PM	"	240	"..............Canutillo........."		7.17AM	"
11.40PM	"	253	Ar.............El Paso...........Lv		7.00AM	"

Equipment

Trains 13 and 14

Chair Car..............Albuquerque and El Paso.

One very interesting passenger train was the *El Pasoan*. In the 1960s, the train often operated with 1 E-8 for power, 1 streamlined Baggage car and 2 Chair Cars. (Spring, 1960 Time Table)

eral train operations. There was a Houston - Oakland Pullman Sleeping thru car service in both directions. Still other Pullmans and Chair Cars operated between the various stations between Texas and California.

The 1966 time table continued to show the *California Special* in both directions with the now Richmond, California terminal as well as Los Angeles. Refer to the time table in this section to view the various through car operations of this complicated train service involving a number of trains including the *Grand Canyon* and the *San Francisco Chief*. See 1960 Time Tables in this chapter for other connections, such as the Angelo.

The *California Special* was no longer designated as a train in the late 1960s timetables.

THE ANTELOPE

The *Antelope* provided a Kansas City - Oklahoma City through Pullman Sleeping Car service in the early 1950s. Trains 27 and 28 connected with the Grand Canyon, trains 123 and 124 at Newton in both directions. The train provided through Chair Car services between Oklahoma City and Kansas City.

The *Antelope* was no longer listed as part of the train services by the mid-1950s.

THE SCOUT

The *Scout* was still another name train with a variety of train connections offering a through Pullman Sleeping Car service between Chicago and Albuquerque in the early 1950s. In fact, a heavy weight Pullman, an 8 Section, 1 Drawing Room and 2 Compartment car operated on the train.

The group of train Numbers Westbound and Eastbound included:

Train #	Origin - Destination
3	Chicago to Kansas City
5	Kansas City to Newton
105	Newton to Belen
114	Belen to Albuquerque
113	Albuquerque to Belen
106	Belen to Newton
6	Newton to Kansas City
4	Kansas City to Chicago

The *Scout*, as a name, was no longer part of the train service operations by the mid-1950s.

THE RANGER

The Santa Fe operated a train known as the *Ranger* in the early 1960s. It connected with train 9 (Overnight from Chicago) at Kansas City for a run as train 5 from Kansas City to Houston. The train provided a Pullman Sleeper from Chicago and Topeka plus Chair Car Service between Kansas City to Houston. Coffee Car Services were provided between Kansas City and Fort Worth. Northbound No. 6 connected with train 20, the Chief at Kansas City Chicago

Table 79a from the January, 1954 timetable illustrates trains 75 and 76, the *California Special* and the *Texan* between Clovis and Brownwood with direct connections with two more sets of trains to Fort Worth and Dallas. What is significant is the 75 and 76 actually traveled over three railroads, the AT&SF plus the Panhandle and Santa Fe and the Gulf Coast and Santa Fe.

Clovis, Lubbock, Sweetwater, Brownwood and Ft. Worth-Dallas

Read down   **Read up**

No. 76 The Texan Daily	Mls.	Table 79a	No. 75 California Special Daily
PM	Centr	al Standard Time–A. T. & S. F. Ry.	AM
....	.0	Lv. Clovis, N. Mex.7, 10a, 80. Ar	10.50	....
		P. & S. F. Ry.	
4.25	9.4	" .Farwell-Texico, N. Mex. Lv	10.30
f 4.38	19.0	" ......Lariat, Tex......... "	f 10.15
5.00	31.4	" ......Muleshoe......... "	9.57
5.23	47.3	" ......Sudan......... "	9.30
5.34	54.7	" ......Amherst......... "	9.15
5.55	62.2	" ......Littlefield......... "	9.00
6.10	74.8	" ......Anton......... "	8.33
6.32	87.3	" ......Shallowater......... "	8.12
7.00	98.9	Ar......Lubbock 10a,79,86,87,88. Lv	7.45
7.15	98.9	Lv......Lubbock......... Ar	7.30
7.35	114.3	Ar......Slaton 89......... Lv	7.05
7.40	114.3	Lv......Slaton......... Ar	7.00
f 7.50	121.6	" ......Southland......... Lv	
8.07	138.1	" ......Post......... "	6.27
f 8.23	153.3	" ......Justiceburg......... "	
f 8.41	171.1	" ......Dermott......... "	
8.55	181.2	" ......Snyder......... "	5.40
f 9.10	192.9	" ......Hermleigh......... "	
9.40	220.4	Ar......Sweetwater 78......... Lv	4.50
		G. C & S. F. Ry.	
9.50	220.4	Lv......Sweetwater......... Ar	4.30
12.25	335.0	ArBrownwood10a,64,66,67,71 Lv	2.00
No. 78			**No. 77**
12.50	335.0	Lv......Brownwood......... Ar	1.35
5.45	473.8	Ar....Ft. Worth 64, 65, 67. Lv	9.20
No. 111			**No. 112**
7.00	473.8	Lv....Ft. Worth......... Ar	9.00
7.45	504.8	Ar....Dallas......... Lv	8.15
AM			PM

No. 112-77-75 and No. 76-78-111 carry Air-conditioned 6 Roomette, 6 Sec., 4 D. B. R. Pullman and chair car between Clovis and Dallas-Ft. Worth.

THE GRAND CANYON–(Southern Section)

Trains 23 and 24 Via Amarillo and Clovis

Chicago, Kansas City, Ottawa Jct., Phoenix
Grand Canyon, Los Angeles and San Francisco

Non-extra-fare, Pullman and Chair Car Service.

Courier-nurse (on Pullman Section).

Dormitory-Lounge Car.....Chicago and Los Angeles.

Sleeping Car.............Chicago and Los Angeles—14 Sections.
Chicago and Los Angeles—10 Roomettes., 3 D. B. R., 2 Comps.
Chicago and Los Angeles (via Grand Canyon)—8 Section, D. R., 2 Comps. (On No. 123 and 124 between Grand Canyon and Los Angeles.)
Chicago and Oakland—6 Section, 6 Roomettes, 4 D. B. R. (On No. 61 and 60 between Bakersfield and Oakland.)
New Orleans and Oakland—6 Sec., 6 Roomettes, 4 D. B. R. (On Mo. Pac. No. 3 to Houston thence No. 66-75 to Clovis, on No. 23-61 Barstow to Oakland; On No. 60-24 Oakland to Clovis, on No. 76-65 from Clovis to Houston thence Mo. Pac. No. 4 to New Orleans).
Dallas-Ft. Worth and Los Angeles—6 Sec., 6 Roomettes, 4 D.B.R. (On No. 112-77-75 Dallas to Clovis; on No. 76-78-111, Clovis to Dallas).
Barstow to Oakland—10 Sec., D. R., 2 Comps.—Westbound only. (On No. 3 from Chicago).

Dining Car..............Chicago and Los Angeles. Barstow and Oakland (Fred Harvey Service). Breakfast from $1.20; Dinner from $2.20. Also a la carte service.

Club Car................Los Angeles to San Diego. San Diego to Fullerton. (On connecting train).

Chair Car...............Chicago and Oakland. (On No. 61 and 60 between Bakersfield and Oakland.) Chicago and Los Angeles. Kansas City and Los Angeles, Dallas and Los Angeles. (On No. 112-77-75 Dallas to Clovis; on No. 76-78-111 Clovis to Dallas).
(All chair car seats reserved between Chicago-San Francisco, Chicago-Los Angeles, Kansas City-Los Angeles; and ALL intermediate points.) Grand Canyon chair car passengers change at Williams.
Chair Car ready for early occupancy at Williams.

THE GRAND CANYON–(Northern Section)

Trains 23-123 and 124-24 Via La Junta and Albuquerque

Chicago, Kansas City, Topeka,
Grand Canyon, Los Angeles and San Francisco

Non-extra-fare Pullman and Chair Car Service.

No Courier-Nurse Service on this train.

Dormitory-Lounge Car .....Chicago and Los Angeles.

Sleeping Car ....Chicago and Los Angeles—8 Sec., D. R., 2 Comps.
Grand Canyon and Los Angeles—8 Sec., D. R., 2 Comps.
Kansas City and Denver—6 Section, 6 Roomettes, 4 D. B. R. (On No. 1-102 La Junta to Denver; on No. 101-2 Denver to La Junta).
Denver and Los Angeles—6 Section, 6 Roomettes, 4 D. B. R. (On No. 141-14 Denver to La Junta; No. 13-130 La Junta to Denver).

Dining Car..............Chicago and Los Angeles. Barstow and Oakland (Fred Harvey Service). Breakfast from $1.20; Luncheon a la carte; Dinner from $2.20.

Club Car................Los Angeles to San Diego. San Diego to Fullerton. (On connecting train).

Chair Car...............Chicago and Los Angeles. Kansas City and Denver. (On No. 1-102 La Junta to Denver; on No. 101-2 Denver to La Junta).
(All chair car seats reserved between Chicago-Los Angeles, Kansas City-Denver, Denver-Los Angeles, and ALL intermediate points.) Denver and Los Angeles (On No. 141-14 Denver to La Junta; on No. 13-130 La Junta to Denver).
Grand Canyon chair car passengers change at Williams.
Chair Car ready for early occupancy at Williams.

passengers. Trains 9 and 6 did not carry the name *Ranger* during the mid-1950s. The 1960 time table listed the train service with the name.

THE ANGELO

The *Angelo* was listed in the 1960 time table providing Chair Car service between Dallas-Fort Worth and San Angelo, a distance of 263 miles. The train connected with trains 111 and 112 at Fort Worth, and operated as trains 77 and 78 between Fort Worth and San Angelo. The name *Angelo* was no longer carried in the timetables as a train name by the mid-1960s.

There is no doubt about it! The Santa Fe operated an incredible number of passenger trains for the traveling public throughout its career. The company had a high rate of return passengers / travelers right up until the dwindling of passenger patronage nationwide. And the name trains were only part of the picture. Santa Fe passenger services are truly a subject of several books with many lessons for service in the 21st Century.

The *Grand Canyon* literally deserves a book all itself. This train was part of the transcontinental train services with one of the widest variety of train service points. Looking through the equipment listings for both the Southern and Northern sections, one can find pairs of stations, such as Oakland and New Orleans, that one would not really expect to find on a primary Chicago – Los Angeles train. (January, 1954 Time Table)

What more could one ask for with the "Romance" of railroading, and especially with the extensive Santa Fe passenger services. It is March 28, 1946, and a triple header with steam power numbers 3872, 934 and 3718 are leaving Raton, New Mexico with a mail train running as 2nd No. 20. The consist of 15 cars is gaining speed and is up to 25 miles per hour as it passes the photographer. (R. H. Kindig)

The "Streamlined Era" has been expanding for 13 years when this photo of the *Centennial State* was taken at Palmer Lake, Colorado on August 6, 1949. The eight car consist includes one streamlined coach as well as thru a Pullman Sleeper. The train operated as train 9 from Kansas City to Pueblo, and as No. 90 for the remainder of the trip into Denver. Eastbound, the Centennial State operated as train 101 to Colorado Springs, and No. 10 for the remainder of the trip to Kansas City. (1947 Time Tables) (TLC Collection)

Westbound No. 3, the *California Limited* is crossing the old Canyon Diablo Bridge while the new arch span bridge can be seen under construction to the left. Note that there is but one Box Express Car on the head-end of this superb train. (Santa Fe Railway, Kansas State Historical Society Collection)

It is October, 1941, and the *Grand Canyon Limited* has a consist of nearly all streamlined equipment with the exception of the two head-end cars. (Harold K. Vollrath Collection)

It is April 15, 1946, and train No. 1, the *Scout* is rolling along at speed near Hesperia, California with the 3771 on the head-end for power. The train has a mixed consist of streamlined and heavy-weight passenger equipment. (William Barham, David Carlson Collection)

The Streamlined Era is well underway in 1940 as can be observed in this photo of the westbound *Kansas Cityan* powered by the diesel units and 1 and 10, which were later renumbered 83-A and 84-A respectively. All but one of the cars of the 11 car train are streamlined equipment. The train is rolling along at speed on the double track Illinois Division near Chillicothe, Illinois. (TLC Collection)

Train No. 28, the *Antelope*, is rolling by
Chicago Junction at Kansas City on a rather
foggy day in July, 1941. No. 28, along with
train 10 (The *Centennial State*) connected
with the *Grand Canyon Limited*, train No. 24,
at Kansas City for the duration of the trip to
Chicago. (Harold K. Vollrath Collection)

The eastbound counterpart of the *Kansas Cityan* was the *Chicagoan*. This photo by Otto Perry shows No. 12 at Wichita with 7 cars. At Kansas City, it will combine with train 212 for the remainder of the trip to Chicago. It is May 25, 1940. (Denver Public Library, Western History Collection, OP 2140)

Still another 1940 view of train No. 11, the *Kansas Cityan*, this time with a full streamlined consist. The reserved seat train is powered by the E-3 cab unit No. 11 along with a B. This portrait was also taken near Chillicothe, Illinois during the summer time and vacation travel was on track. (TLC Collection)

The Westbound *Kansas Cityan*, west of Monica, Illinois, has a consist of 12 cars with No. 10 for power on the head end just after the War in June, 1946. (Otto Perry, Denver Public Library, Western History Collection, OP 2138)

It is a beautiful Summer day in July, 1963, and train 124 - the *Grand Canyon* - is approaching the Rock Island crossing at Joliet, Illinois. The 15 car train includes 8 head-end cars including a thru Box Express Car for the New York Central and three flat cars with containers with U.S. Mail. The train also includes seven passenger carrying cars including Chair Cars, a Dormitory Lounge, Dining Car, and two Sleeping cars. (William S. Kuba)

By 1969, the Santa Fe had lost much of the U.S. Mail contracts, and the *Grand Canyon* as well as other trains took quite a beating. This May, 1969 photo shows the westbound *Grand Canyon*, train 23 with but two units, one baggage car and Chair Cars only. (William S. Kuba)

The *Navajo*, train No. 10, is making fast time on a foggy day as it rolls east out of Amarillo, Texas. The 9 car train is double headed with the 1313 and the 1312, which are already up to 40 miles per hour and gaining speed on an early Spring day in April, 1937. (Otto Perry, Denver Public Library, Western History Collection, OP 1196)

Train No. 5, the westbound *Ranger*, has a consist of 13 cars as it rolls across Kansas. It is May, 1940 with a cloudy day – still a great day to ride a train or out taking photographs of an incredible rolling history of the Santa Fe passenger train services. (Otto Perry, Denver Public Library, Western History Collection, OP 1564)

A rather unique name for a train was the Fast Fifteen. Although this photo predates the streamline era (August, 1932), we have included this photo of a train with such an interesting name. Train 15 is shown here departing Kansas City. (Otto Perry, Denver Public Library, Western History Collection, OP 1638)

It is a dark with a bit of rain as the *California Limited*, running as 1st No. 4, rolls eastbound just east of Newton, Kansas. Note the green flags depicting a following section (Otto Perry, Denver Public Library, Western History Collection, OP 2161)

The *Grand Canyon*, trains 23 and 24, operated with coaches only during its last days. However, the 1969 and 1970 Summer issue timetables, trains 23 and 24 were listed as having Chair Cars between Chicago and Los Angeles plus a Lunch Counter Dining Car between Chicago and Barstow. A Sleeping Car was also handled on trains 23 and 24 between Barstow and Los Angeles. The Sleeper operated through to Chicago on trains 1 and 2, the *San Francisco Chief*. The timetables also indicated a Lounge Car between Chicago and Barstow during the summer season only. This photo shows a July, 1968 edition with the 403 (U30CG) leading a four consist. (Harold K. Vollrath Collection)

As noted elsewhere, many of the "Non-Chiefs" were also equipped with Observation Chair cars or Observation Parlor Cars as part of the consist. Such equipment provided a superb, streamlined ending for all types of trains. This view shows the rear end of the *Chicagoan*, the daily Kansas City to Chicago Streamliner. The *Chicagoan* was part of the day train service team with the westbound *Kansas Cityan*. The trains operated as 11 and 12 and made the 451 mile run in 7 hours, 25 minutes and 7 hours, 30 minutes respectively in 1954. The trains were equipped with Chair Cars as well as a Dining Car and a Chair Lounge Car. The pair of trains also connected at Kansas City with trains 211 and 212, the *Tulsan*, for Tulsa, Oklahoma. The connecting schedules actually provided a day run in both directions for the 707 miles. Through cars included a Chair Car and the Parlor Observation Car between Chicago and Tulsa according to a 1954 time table. (Santa Fe Railway, Kansas State Historical Society Collection)

The Santa Fe also advertised a variety of other passenger trains on their freight equipment such as the "Scout" on ATSF 40 foot box car 274199. (From the National Archives of Canada, Negative No. PA-185617)

PULLMAN
LINE

(Page 25)

TRAIN 124
LOS ANGELES - WINSLOW

1 Storage Mail	Los Angeles	- Pittsburgh (Sealed) Extra
1 Storage Mail	" "	- Buffalo (Sealed) Extra
1 Storage Mail	" "	- Springfield, Mass. (Sealed) Extra
1 Storage Mail	" "	- New York (WST) (Sealed) Extra
1 Bage-Exp-Mail	" "	- Chicago, Daily
1 Storage Mail	" "	- Fort Worth, Exc. Sun-Mon.)For
1 Bage-Exp-Mail	" "	- Dallas, Daily) 24
1 Bage-Exp-Mail	" "	- Kansas City, Daily)Winslow.
1 Chair	" "	" " (For 23 Winslow)
1 Chair	" "	- Dallas (For 23 Winslow; 76 Clovis)
3 Chairs	" "	- Chicago (6 cars June 1st to Sept. 15th)
1 Diner	" "	- " "
1 Lounge	" "	- " "
..04 1 14-Section	" "	- " "
..01 1 6-1-4	" "	- " "
..13 1 6-6	" "	- Dallas (For 23 Winslow; 76 Clovis)
..48 1 8-1-2	" "	- Kansas City (For 23 Winslow)
..12 1 8-2-2	" "	- Grand Canyon - Chicago (For No. 2 Winslow
..17 1 6-6-4	" "	- " " (June 1st to Sept. 15th)
..17 1 8-1-3	Phoenix - Chicago (Off 42 Ash Fork)	

22 cars Los Angeles to Winslow (21 cars Sun-Mon.)
25 " " " " " " (24 " " ")(June 1 - Sept.1

Grand Canyon, trains 123 and 124, had some real heavy consists during most
...s career. This 1957 snap shot shows 124 with as many as 25 cars with a bal-
...ed mixture of head-end and passenger traffic. Note that the train carried as many
...x Pullman cars departing Los Angeles. Head-end traffic from LA required as
...y as eight cars with four of them headed for eastern destinations. (Santa Fe
...senger Consist, 1957)

PAGE 35

TRAIN 201 LA JUNTA - PUEBLO

1	SM	La Junta-Pueblo Ex Sun
1	EM	Los Angeles-Denver (Off 8 for C&S)
1	BEM	Kansas City-Denver (Off 23 for C&S)
1	CC	La Junta-Pueblo-Denver

TRAIN 190 PUEBLO - LA JUNTA

1	BEM	Denver-Kansas City (Off C&S for)
1	EM	Denver-Albuquerque Ex Sat Sun (Off C&S for 23)
1	EM	Denver-Los Angeles Sat & Sun (Off C&S for 23)
1	EM	Pueblo-Kansas City Ex Sat Sun (For 8)
1	EM	Pueblo-La Junta Sat
1	CC	Denver-Pueblo-La Junta

TRAIN 211 KANSAS CITY - TULSA

1	30-40 Combn	Kansas City-Tulsa
1	BM	Kansas City-Tulsa Ex Sun Mon Tue
2	CC	Kansas City-Tulsa (See Note 1)
1	CC	Chicago-Tulsa (Off 19 KC)

TRAIN 212 TULSA - KANSAS CITY

1	30-40 Combn	Tulsa-Kansas City
1	DH Bag	Tulsa-Kansas City Ex Mon Tue Wed
2	CC	Tulsa-Kansas City (See Note 1)
1	CC	Tulsa-Chicago (For 12 KC)

...E 1 Bag-Chair 3490-91 operated Summer months

...e time 1966 arrived, the trains to and from Denver (201 and 190) in 1966 were
...ly down to one coach but did include a fair amount of head-end traffic. Trains
...and 212, the *Tulsan*, connected with the *Chief* from Chicago, and the
...agoan, No. 12 to Chicago at Kansas City. Note the thru Chair Car from No.
...and for No. 12 to and from the Windy City. (Santa Fe Passenger Consist, 1966)

PULLMAN
LINE

(Page 18)

TRAINS 191-190
LA JUNTA - DENVER

1 Express-Mail	Kansas City - Denver, Exc. Sun-Mon-Tue. (Off Train 7
1 Express-Mail	La Junta - Denver, Sun-Mon-Tue.
1 Baggage	" " - " , Daily
1 LCD	" " - " "
1 Chair	Chicago - Denver
1 Chair	Los Angeles - Denver
4510 1 6-6-4	" " - " "
4523 1 6-6-4	Chicago - Denver
1 Chair	La Junta - Denver

8 cars La Junta to Denver.

TRAINS 201-200
DENVER - LA JUNTA

1 Express-Mail	Denver - Los Angeles, Daily)For
1 Bage-Exp-Mail	" " - Albuquerque, ")123
1 LCD	" " - La Junta
1 Chair	" " - Chicago
1 Chair	" " - Los Angeles
4510 1 6-6-4	" " - " "
4523 1 6-6-4	" " - Chicago
1 Chair	" " - La Junta

8 cars Denver to La Junta.

The connections to and from Denver, trains 191-190 and 201-200 consisted of
eight cars during their career in 1957. (Santa Fe Passenger Consist, 1957)

PULLMAN
LINE

(Page 33)

TRAINS 77-78
BROWNWOOD - SAN ANGELO - BROWNWOOD

1 Bage-Exp-Mail	Dallas - San Angelo, Daily
1 30-40' Combn.	Fort Worth - San Angelo, Daily
1 Chair	" " " - " " "

3 cars Brownwood to San Angelo to Brownwood

TRAIN 78
BROWNWOOD - FORT WORTH

1 Storage Mail	Los Angeles - Fort Worth, Exc. Tues-Wed.)
1 Bage-Exp-Mail	" " - Dallas, Daily)Off
1 Storage Mail	Lubbock - Dallas, Exc. Monday)For 111)76
1 Bage-Exp-Mail	" " - Fort Worth, Daily)
1 Bage-Exp-Mail	San Angelo - Dallas, Daily (For 111)
1 30-40' Combn.	" " - Fort Worth, Daily
1 Chair	" " - " "
1 Chair	Los Angeles - Dallas (Off 76 Brownwood)
4513 1 6-6	" " - " " (" ")

8 cars Brownwood to Fort Worth (Mon-Tues-Wed.)
9 " " " " " (Thur-Fri-Sat-Sun.)

TRAINS 211-212
KANSAS CITY - TULSA - KANSAS CITY

1 30-40' Combn. (LW)	Kansas City - Tulsa - Kansas City, Daily
2 Chairs	" " " - " - " "
1 Lounge-Diner	" " " - " - " "
1 Chair	" " " - " - " "

5 cars Kansas City to Tulsa to Kansas City

TRAINS 311-312
NEWTON - DODGE CITY - NEWTON

1 Baggage-Express (LW)	Newton - Dodge City - Newton, Daily
1 Chair	" " - " - "

2 cars Newton to Dodge City to Newton

This particular consist page from the 1957 assignments shows 211 and 212
with their round trip assignment of 5 cars in each direction. Trains 311 and
312 at the bottom of the sheet operated as 312 out of Dodge City in the early
morning en route to Newton. No. 311 departed Newton in the evening returning to Dodge City. It is another example of some of the shorter trains operated by the Santa Fe during the 1950s/60s.
Trains 77 and 78 provided a connection with trains 111 and 112 at Fort Worth.
This consist sheet illustrates the 3 car consist between Brownwood and San
Angelo as well as the thru operation of 78 with the thru equipment between
Los Angeles and Fort Worth. (Santa Fe Passenger Consist, 1957)

Chapter 4 - LOCAL AND BRANCH LINE PASSENGER SERVICES

The Santa Fe, as with many North American railroads, offered an extensive local and branch line passenger services on many routes. There were also many local passenger trains operating over the main lines providing service for many short run passengers. This also included passengers from thru trains, who could detrain at one location, and then catch a local train to their final destination. Or the other way around with one boarding a local and then detraining at a thru train station stop to change trains. Such service opened up many avenues for smaller towns and cities. In a sense, the locals were actually providing a hub type of a service.

The local trains were equipped with either short train consists, such as one or two head-end cars with one or two coaches. Sometimes the trains included sleeping cars, especially for branch line operations and other market areas. Many trains were two car trains, while a host of others were equipped with Gas-electric Doodle Bug cars.

The local trains began to disappear shortly after the end of the World War II era. However, the Santa Fe carefully scrutinized which locals provided the greatest benefits for the traveling public. The company realized with its philosophy that many of the local trains fed the long distance trains, not only for passengers, but also a certain amount of mail and express business. Just one example of a passenger exchange could be found on the main line from Chicago. In the early 1950s, train 23, the Grand Canyon, departed Chicago at 12:30 p.m. and arrived at Streator at 2:10 p.m. No. 23 made but two stops over the next 145 miles at Chillicothe and Galesburg before reaching Ft. Madison. Passengers en route to stations between Streator and Ft. Madison could detrain at Streator and board the local No. 25, which made all stops to Ft. Madison.

The remainder of this chapter is devoted to a variety of photos, local train listings, and other information regarding this incredible piece of service; which was basically lost to the automobile. Two periods of time are covered: the early 1950s and the early 1960s. Actually many of the local trains disappeared during the late 1920s and 30s, and some were even discontinued during the War Years because of the need for equipment and motive power for troop movements and other heavy duty passenger traffic during that period of time. However, the early 1950s was basically the last era for such passenger services throughout North America. As of 2004, one can only really find local passenger trains in the City-Suburban Commuter Rail Services, which fortunately is expanding faster than ever. However that is another story.

Many of the branch line passenger trains and a variety of local main line runs were handled by Gas-electric cars, such as the M-115 in this photo. The M-115 was a combination Coach and could handle baggage and express as well as mail sorting in the Rail Post Office section of the car. The M-115 was built by Electro-Motive and its portrait was taken at Amarillo, Texas in February, 1961. The fleet of Gas-electrics was truly the backbone for much of the local and branch line operations. (Harold K. Vollrath Collection)

The Early 1950s

The following information includes the train numbers and if the train was a mixed train or equipped with a Gas-Electric, referred to as a "Motor" car in the time tables. Full passenger trains are listed as "Passenger".

Train Numbers	Route	Equipment	Frequency
13 - 14	Chicago and Ancona	Gas-electric	Daily Except Sun.
25 - 26	Streator and Fort Madison	Gas-electric	Daily Except Sun.
28	Newton to Kansas City	Passenger	Daily
		The Antelope	
51 - 52	Emporia and Strong City	Gas-electric	Daily Except Sun.
55 - 56	Emporia and Strong City	Mixed Train	Sun. Only
57 - 58	Fort Madison and Kansas City	Gas-electric	Daily
3 - 4	Dodge City and Holly	Passenger	Daily
		California Limited	
70 - 75	Los Angeles and San Diego	Passenger	Daily
7 - 6	Bakersfield and Oakland	Passenger	Daily
105 - 106	Dodge City and Albuquerque	Passenger	Daily
13 - 14	Albuquerque and El Paso	Passenger	Daily
13 - 14	Streator and Pekin, Illinois	Gas-electric	Daily Except Sun.
47 - 42	Ash Fork and Phoenix	Passenger	Daily
117 - 118	Cadiz and Phoenix	Passenger	Daily
47 - 48	Kansas City and Tulsa	Passenger	Daily
97 - 198	Moline to Emporia via Virgil	Mixed	Daily
	Daily Except Saturday between		
	Virgil and M. D. Junction		
98	Emporia to Moline	Mixed	Daily
	Returned as 97		
73 - 74	Lawrence and Ottawa	Mixed	Daily Except Sun.
43 - 44	Henrietta and St. Joseph	Mixed	Daily Except Sun.
63 - 64	Chanute and Longton	Mixed	Daily Except Sun.
77 - 78	Chanute and Pittsburg	Mixed	Daily Except Sun.
	Ferry Service between Pittsburg		
	And Joplin		
67 - 68	Coffeyville and Cherryvale	Mixed	67 Daily Except Sun.
			68 Daily Except Sat.
113 - 114	Coffeyville and Newton	Motor	Daily
55 - 56	St. Joseph and Topeka	Motor	Daily Except Sun.
79 - 80	Ottawa and Gridley	Mixed	Daily Except Sun.
83 - 84	Holliday and Leavenworth	Mixed	Daily Except Sun.
51 - 52	Burlingame and Alma	Mixed	Daily Except Sun.
25 - 26	Emporia and Winfield	Motor	Daily
51 - 52	Emporia and Concordia	Motor	Daily Except Sun.
55 - 56	Emporia and Concordia	Mixed	Sun. Only
73 - 74	Strong City, Abilene and Superior	Mixed	Daily Except Sun.
93 - 94	Hutchinson and Ponca City	Motor	Daily
69 - 70	Attica and Belvidere	Mixed	Daily Except Sun.
41 - 42	Waynoka and Buffalo	Mixed	Daily Except Sun.
79 - 80	Geuda Springs and South Haven	Mixed	Tue. Thur. Sat.
79 - 80	Abilene, Salina and Osborne	Mixed	Daily Except Sun.
77 - 78	South Haven and Anthony	Mixed	77 Tue. Thur. Sat.
			78 Mon. Wed. Fri.
85 - 86	Manchester and Barnard	Mixed	Tue. Thur. Sat.
47 - 48	Wichita and Englewood	Motor	Daily
69 - 70	Scott City and Garden City	Mixed	69 Mon. Wed. Fri.
			70 Tue. Thur. Sat.
69 - 70	Great Bend and Scott City	Mixed	Daily Except Sun.
87 - 88	Florence and Ellinwood	Mixed	Daily Except Sun.
89 - 90	Little River and Galatia	Mixed	Daily Except Sun.
71 - 72	Larned and Jetmore	Mixed	71 Mon. Wed. Fri.
			72 Tue. Thur. Sat.
73 - 74	Dodge City and Boise City	Mixed	Daily Except Sun.
85 - 86	Satanta and Pritchett	Mixed	85 Mon. Wed. Fri.
			86 Tue. Thur. Sat.

85 - 86	Holly and La Junta	Mixed	85 Tue. Thur. Sat.
			86 Mon. Wed. Fri.
71 - 72	Independence and Ralston	Mixed	Daily Except Sun.
80 - 87	Cushing to Guthrie	Mixed	Daily Except Sun.
88 - 79	Guthrie to Cushing		
59 - 60	Drumright and Cushing	Mixed	Daily Except Sun.
39 - 40	Moriarty and Willard	Mixed	Wed. Sat.
51 - 52	Arkansas City and Shawnee	Motor	Daily
305 - 306	Shawnee and South Shawnee	Motor	Daily Except Sun.
47 - 48	Rincon and Silver City	Mixed	Daily
37 - 38	La Junta and Boise City	Mixed	Daily
57 - 56	Whitewater and Hurley	Mixed	Daily
55 - 58	Whitewater and Santa Rita	Mixed	Daily
93 - 94	Lamy and Santa Fe	Mixed	Daily Except Sun.
53 - 54	Hanover Junction and Fierro	Mixed	Daily
43 - 44	Socorro and Magdalena	Mixed	Daily Except Sun.
14 - 15	Williams and Grand Canyon	Passenger	Daily
25 - 26	Prescott and Blue Bell	Mixed	Mon. Wed. Fri.
25 - 26	Rice and Blythe	Mixed	25 Daily Except Mon.
			26 Daily Except Sun.
51 - 54	San Bernardino and Los Angeles	Passenger	Daily
5 - 6	Fort Worth and Galveston	Passenger	Daily
	Long Distance Local		
73 - 74	Temple and Brownwood	Motor	Daily
77 - 78	Brownwood and San Angelo	Passenger	Daily
53 - 54	Lometa and Eden	Mixed	53 Sun. Tue. Thur.
			54 Mon. Wed. Fri.
310 - 311	Ardmore and Ringling	Mixed	Daily Except Sun.
67 - 68	Paris and Dallas	Motor	Daily
201 - 202	Beaumont and Longview	Motor	Daily
81 - 82	Brownwood and Menard	Motor	Daily
115 - 116	Sealy and Matagorda	Mixed	Daily Except Sun.
109 - 110	Eagle Lake and Garwood	Mixed	Daily Except Sun.
301- 302	Pauls Valley and Lindsay	Mixed	301 Mon. Wed. Fri.
			302 Tue. Thur. Sat.
86-85	Ada to Pauls Valley	Mixed	Daily Except Sun.
85-86	Pauls Valley to Ada	Mixed	Daily Except Sun.
305 - 306	Shawnee and Lindsay	Motor	Daily Except Sun.
45 - 46	Wichita and San Angelo	Motor	Daily
129 - 130	San Angelo and Fort Stockton	Mixed	Daily
129 - 130	Fort Stockton and Presidio	Mixed	129 Tue. Thur. Sun.
			130 Mon. Wed. Fri.
5 - 6	Houston and Temple	Passenger	Daily
73 - 74	Temple and Brownwood	Motor	Daily
75 - 76	Brownwood and Clovis	Passenger	Daily
25 -26	Clovis and Carlsbad	Passenger	Daily
45 - 46	Carlsbad and Pecos	Mixed	45 Mon. Wed. Fri.
			46 Tue. Thur. Sat.
39 - 40	Shattuck and Spearman	Motor	Daily Except Sun.
61 - 62	Pampa and Clinton	Mixed	61 Mon. Wed. Fri.
			62 Tue. Thur. Sat.
57 - 58	White Deer and Skellytown	Mixed	Daily Except Sun.
59 - 60	Panhandle and Borger	Mixed	Daily Except Sun.
81 - 82	Plainview and Floydada	Mixed	Daily
89 - 90	Lubbock and Crosbytown	Mixed	Daily Except Sun.
79 - 80	Lubbock and Bledsoe	Mixed	Daily Except Sun.
77 - 78	Lubbock and Seagraves	Mixed	Daily Except Sun.
83 - 84	Slaton and Lamesa	Mixed	Daily Except Sun.
127 - 128	San Angelo and Sonora	Mixed	Daily Except Sun.
93 - 96	Amarillo and Lubbock	Passenger	Daily
78 - 77	Slaton and Sweetwater	Passenger	Daily
	(Provides connections for Pullman and coach service between Clovis and Dallas.)		

As one can see from the list, there was quite an extensive local train service in operation on the Santa Fe System through the early

51

1950s. This would change dramatically over the next decade into the 1960s. The next listing shows the locals and branch line services in operation during the early 1960s.

The Early 1960s

Train Numbers	Route	Equipment	Frequency
123 - 124	Chicago - Kansas City The Grand Canyon provided a partial local service over various segments between Chicago and Kansas City	Passenger	Daily
311 - 312	Newton and Dodge City	Passenger	Daily
7	Bakersfield and Richmond One direction only	Passenger	Daily
47 - 48	Kansas City and Tulsa	Passenger	Daily
13 - 14	Albuquerque and El Paso	Passenger	Daily
43 - 44	Henrietta and St. Joseph	Mixed	Daily Except Sun.
185 - 186	Satanta and Pritchett	Mixed	185 Sun. Tue. Thur. 186 Mon. Wed. Fri.
37 - 38	Las Animas Junction and Amarillo	Mixed	Daily
73 - 74	Concordia and Superior	Mixed	73 Mon. Wed. Fri. 74 Tue. Thur. Sat.
73 - 74	Strong City and Concordia	Mixed	Daily Except Sun.
25 - 26	Clovis and Carlsbad	Passenger	Daily
77-82	Geuda Springs to Harper	Mixed	Tue. Thur. Sat.
81-78	Harper to Geuda Springs	Mixed	Mon. Wed. Fri.
79 - 80	Geuda Springs and South Haven	Mixed	79 Mon. Wed. Fri. 80 Tue. Thur. Sat.
85 - 86	Manchester and Barnard	Mixed	Wed. Fri.
89 - 90	Little River and Galatia	Mixed	Tue. Fri.
59-60	Hutchinson to Wellington	Mixed	Tue. Thur. Sat.
57-58	Wellington to Hutchinson	Mixed	Mon. Wed. Fri.
77 - 78	Chanute and Pittsburg	Mixed	Daily Except Sun.
67 - 68	Wichita and Pratt	Mixed	Daily Except Sun.
71 - 72	Wichita and Englewood	Mixed	71 Mon. Wed. Fri. 72 Tue. Thur. Sat.
69 - 70	Attica and Belvidere	Mixed	Daily Except Sun.
79 - 80	Abilene and Osborne	Mixed	79 Mon. Wed. Fri. 80 Tue. Thur. Sat.
69 - 70	Scott City and Garden City	Mixed	Daily Except Sun.
173 - 174	Dodge City and Boise City	Mixed	173 Mon. Wed. Fri. 174 Tue. Thur. Sat.
77 - 78	Fort Worth and San Angelo	Passenger	Daily
75 - 76	Temple and Clovis	Passenger	Daily
\85 - 86	Holly and La Junta	Mixed	85 Tue. Thur. Sat. 86 Mon. Wed. Fri.
93 - 94	Amarillo and Lubbock	Passenger	Daily
61 - 62	Pampa and Clinton	Mixed	61 Mon. Wed. Fri. 62 Tue. Thur. Sat.
59 - 60	Panhandle and Borger	Mixed	Daily Except Sun.
77 - 78	Wellington and South Haven	Mixed	77 Tue. Thur. Sat. 78 Mon. Wed. Fri.
57 - 50	Wellington and Blackwell	Mixed	57 Mon. Wed. Fri. 50 Tue. Thur. Sat.

Moving forward now to 1969, many of the trains listed above had been discontinued. Some of the main line trains, such as 23 and 24, the Grand Canyon, were assigned local services on various segments of the route. For 23 and 24, this pretty much the case for the entire distance between Chicago and Los Angeles. The local passenger trains still in operation in 1969 were as follows:

The Late 1960s

Train Numbers	Route	Equipment	Frequency
43 - 44	Henrietta and St. Joseph	Mixed	Daily Except Sun.
185 - 186	Satanta and Pritchett	Mixed	185 Sun. Tue. Thur. 186 Mon. Wed. Fri.
173 - 174	Dodge City and Boise City	Passenger	173 Mon. Wed. Fri. 174 Tue. Thur. Sat.
CWT - WTC	Las Animas Junction and Boise City	Mixed	Daily Freight Train Symbol
73 - 74	Strong City and Concordia	Mixed	Daily Except Sunday
73 - 74	Concordia and Superior	Mixed	73 Mon. Wed. Fri. 74 Tue. Thur. Sat.
85 - 86	Manchester and Barnard	Mixed	Tue. Thur.
89 - 90	Little River and Galatia	Mixed	Tue. Fri.
77 - 78	Chanute and Pittsburg	Mixed	Daily Except Sun.
79 - 80	Abilene and Osborne	Mixed	79 Mon. Wed. Fri. 80 Tue. Thur. Sat.
85 - 86	Holly and Swink	Mixed	85 Tue. Thur. Sat. 86 Mon. Wed. Fri.
59 - 60	Wellington and Tonkawa	Mixed	59 Tue. Thur. Sat. 60. Mon. Wed. Fri.

The Mixed train services disappeared over the next 18 months into 1971 and the start up of Amtrak. Although local services were fairly extensive 20 years previously, the chapter was over as far as such trains were concerned on the Santa Fe. However, it must be pointed out that such trains lasted much longer on the Santa Fe than most other railroad passenger services. The Santa Fe locals and mixed trains were indeed a remarkable fleet and along with the many streamliners and other passenger services, there was (and is) much to learn from the marketing approach by this incredible western railroad.

This photo of Gas-electric M-106 at Wichita dates back to April, 1936, the year the Streamlined Era began with the new Super Chief. During that year, there were two sets of local passenger trains equipped with Gas-electrics. Train 47 departed Wichita in the morning with a mid-afternoon arrival in Englewood. The Gas-electric laid over for about 90 minutes and then return to Wichita as train No. 48.

A more complex schedule involved trains 45 and 46, which ran from Wichita all the way to San Angelo, Texas, a distance of 510.4 miles. The 1936 schedule for train 45 was about 16 hours, with a nearly 17 hour schedule from 46 from San Angelo to Wichita. The M-106 was built by General Electric in 1913. (Harold K. Vollrath Collection)

The Gas-electric M-125 carried safety stripes on the front end when this photo was taken in 1936. It was a combination Baggage, Rail Post Office and Coach and could handle a trailer car. At that time, the M-125 was assigned to trains 67 and 68 between Cleburne and Paris and return daily. The M-125 is shown here at Dallas on its daily assignment. (Harold K. Vollrath Collection)

This photo of No. M-125 was taken at DeRidder, Louisiana in July, 1946. Note the change in the paint scheme in 1946 as compared to its 1936 photo. This car operated on trains 291 and 292 between Kirbyville, Texas and Oakdale, Louisiana on the Gulf Coast and Santa Fe Railway. The 82.3 Mile run took about 3 hours in each direction. The M-125 was built by Electro-Motive in 1929. (Harold K. Vollrath Collection)

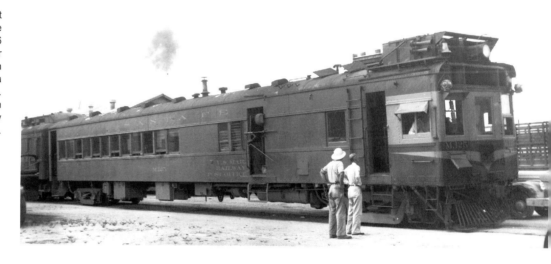

Gas-electric M-153 was a combination Baggage and Rail Post Office without any coach seating. The Gas-electric could handle one or two passenger cars. As one can observe, there is a baggage car coupled to the rear of the M-153, which is shown here at Kirbyville, Texas in September, 1952. The car was assigned to trains 201 and 202 daily between Longview and Beaumont, a distance of 207.9 miles. 201 was scheduled for 8 hours, 5 minutes while train 202 did the run in 8 hours, 15 minutes. The M-153 was built by Electro-Motive in 1931. (Harold K. Vollrath Collection)

Wichita and Presidio

No. 23 Daily	No. 23 Daily	Mls.	Table **78** Central Standard Time	No. 24 Daily	No. 6 Daily
AM	AM			PM	AM
11.00	11.00	.0	Lv...CHICAGO......Ar	6.00	9.00
No. 27	**No. 27**			**No. 28**	
10.00	10.00	451.1	"...KANSAS CITY...Lv	7.25	10.15
3.10	3.10	663.4	Ar...WICHITA.....Lv	2.15	5.10
No. 47	**No. 45**			**No. 46**	**No. 48**
Daily Motor	Daily Motor			Daily Motor	Daily Motor
6.00	5.40	.0	LvWICHITA 4, 7, 23, 32, 33, 64 Ar	11.40	6.05
f 6.20	f 5.53	7.2	"....Prospect....Lv	f11.13	f 4.41
f 6.30	f 5.57	9.7	"....Schulte....	f11.09	f 4.37
6.42	f 6.07	15.9	"....Clonmel....	f11.00	f 4.28
AM	6.20	23.3	"....Viola 33....	10.49	f 4.16
Ar	6.35	31.5	"....Milton....	10.32	PM
	f 6.49	42.1	"..Runnymede..	f10.12	
	7.00	49.2	"..Harper 7, 31..	9.58	
	7.22	61.0	"..Attica 7, 34..	9.35	
	7.30	67.6	"....Crisfield 7..	f 9.21	
	7.40	75.2	"...Hazelton 7...	f 9.05	
	7.55	82.3	"..Kiowa, Kan. 7, 48..	8.50	
	8.26	102.2	"..Cherokee, Okla..	8.10	
	8.43	108.0	"....Yewed....	7.59	
	8.58	116.4	"....Carmen....	7.42	
	9.07	121.2	"....Aline....	7.33	
	9.19	128.5	"...West Cleo...	7.19	
	9.25	131.7	"....Orienta....	7.12	
	9.38	137.9	Ar...FAIRVIEW...Lv	7.00	
	9.45	137.9	Lv...FAIRVIEW...Ar	6.55	
	10.10	149.5	"....Longdale...Lv	6.33	
	10.22	155.9	"....Canton....	6.17	
	10.44	166.9	"....Oakwood....	5.59	
	11.10	180.7	"....Thomas....	5.31	
	11.30	189.9	"...Custer City...	5.10	
	11.41	197.1	"....Arapaho....	4.57	
	12.02	202.7	"...Clinton 82...	4.44	
	12.42	221.8	"....Dill City....	3.56	
	12.56	229.6	"....Sentinel....	3.42	
	1.16	242.8	"...Lone Wolf...	3.22	
	1.28	250.2	"....Lugert....	3.10	
	1.44	259.2	"....Blair....	2.56	
	||2.00	269.2	Ar....ALTUS....Lv	2.40	
	2.30	269.2	Lv....ALTUS....Ar	2.30	
	2.49	280.1	"...Elmer, Okla...Lv	2.10	
			Okla.-Tex. State Line-(P. & S. F. Ry.)		
	f 2.57	285.0	"..Ranchland, Tex..	f 2.01	
	3.06	290.2	"....Odell....	1.52	
	3.24	299.4	"...Chillicothe...	1.35	
	3.35	306.2	"..Medicine Mound...	1.22	
	3.53	316.5	"....Margaret....	1.01	
	4.05	323.2	"....Crowell....	12.46	
	4.18	331.0	"....Foard City....	12.30	
	4.33	340.3	"....Truscott....	12.11	
	4.57	353.0	"....Benjamin....	11.47	
	5.18	365.0	"....Knox City....	11.27	
	5.22	367.6	"....O'Brien....	11.23	
	5.30	372.4	"....Rochester....	11.15	
	5.48	382.0	"....Rule....	11.00	
	6.03	390.3	"....Sagerton....	10.48	
	6.35	407.7	Ar....HAMLIN....Lv	10.20	
	6.40	407.7	Lv....HAMLIN....Ar	10.15	
	6.56	416.2	"...McCaulley...Lv	10.01	
	7.05	421.0	"....Sylvester....	9.52	
	7.18	428.4	"...Longworth...	9.41	
	7.55	442.0	Ar.SWEETWATER 67, 79 Lv	9.15	
	8.00	442.0	Lv..SWEETWATER..Ar	8.30	
	8.32	459.2	"....Maryneal...Lv	8.05	
	9.02	472.9	"....Blackwell....	7.40	
	f 9.12	479.4	"..Ft. Chadbourne..	f 7.30	
No. 145 Daily Motor	9.25	487.2	"....Bronte....	7.19	**No. 146** Daily Motor
	9.42	497.4	"...Tennyson...	7.04	
	9.53	504.0	"....Wooland....	6.55	
AM	10.20	519.3	Ar..SAN ANGELO..{Lv	6.20	PM
8.00	PM	519.3	Lv 66, 67, 72, 90 {Ar	AM	6.10
8.27		534.3	"....Tankersly....Lv		5.43
8.50	**129** Mixed	547.6	"....Mertzon....		5.22
9.28		573.5	"....Barnhart....		4.40
9.59	Leave	592.5	"....Big Lake....		4.07
10.14	Tues.	602.6	"....Best....		3.50
f10.19	Thurs.	604.7	"....Rita Santa....	f	3.45
10.24	Sun.	606.7	"....Texon....		3.38
10.50	Arrive	621.8	"....Rankin....		3.17
11.25	Presi-	640.5	Ar...McCAMEY...Lv		2.45
11.25	dio on	640.5	Lv...McCAMEY...Ar	**130** Mixed	2.45
11.45	Wed.	651.5	Lv....Girvin....Lv	Mon.	2.23
f11.58	Fri.	658.9	"....Owego....	Wed.	f 2.10
f12.10	Mon.	665.7	"....Baldridge....	Fri.	f 1.58
12.40	PM	683.6	Ar..FORT STOCKTON..Lv	PM	1.30
PM	5.30	683.6	Lv..FORT STOCKTON..Ar	11.00	PM
	f 6.55	719.1	"....Hovey....	f 9.37	
	8.45	746.9	Ar....ALPINE....Lv	8.35	
	8.45	746.9	Lv....ALPINE....Ar	7.50	
	f 9.25	758.8	"....Paisano....Lv	f 7.10	
	f10.23	786.4	"....Perdiz....	f 6.10	
	f10.46	795.6	"....Plata....	f 5.45	
	f11.15	804.6	"...Casa-Piedra...	f 5.25	
	12.15	828.6	Ar...PRESIDIO...Lv	4.30	
	AM		*(Rio Grande River)*	PM	

One of the longest local passenger schedules in the January, 1947 timetable, Table 78; on the Santa Fe were trains 45 and 46, a Gas-electric operation, between Wichita and San Angelo, a distance of 519.3 miles. Still other Gas-electrics operated out of San Angelo, such as trains 145 and 146, which operated as a turn to and from Fort Stockton. Beyond Stockton, we have a mixed train operation between to Presidio. (January, 1947 Timetable)

Gas-electric M-183 was also a combination Coach-Baggage and RPO car. This car had a larger bagg compartment but with a smaller coach section. During the late 1940s, M-183 was assigned to trains 57 58 between Topeka and St. Joseph. 57 made the run from St. Joseph to Topeka in 2 hours, 25 minutes, No. 58 did the run in 2 hours, 20 minutes. The M-183 is shown here at Topeka in December, 1949. (Ha K. Vollrath Collection)

Some interesting changes took place with some of the Gas-electrics. M-190, which was an articulated p unit with a baggage car, was rebuilt with diesel power. It was painted in the Santa Fe silver and red scheme. In this January, 1961 photo, the M-190 is at Clovis, New Mexico. It was assigned to trains 25 26 between Carlsbad and Clovis. It connected with the San Francisco Chief at Clovis, and it was equip with a streamlined coach. In this case, the train was a step up from the usual Gas-electric assignment far color schemes and coach accommodations. (Harold K. Vollrath Collection)

Panhandle and Borger

d down	P. & S. F. Ry.	Read up
Mls.	Table **84**	60 Ex.Su. Mixed
	Central Standard Time	PM
.0	Lv......Panhandle 7.....Ar	2.30
28.9	Ar........Borger........Lv	1.00

Plainview and Floydada

d down	P. & S. F. Ry.	Read up
Mls.	Table **85**	82 Daily Mixed
	Central Standard Time	AM
.0	Lv......Plainview 79.... Ar	5.45
15.9	"......Lockney......Lv	5.05
26.6	Ar......Floydada......Lv	4.30
		AM

Lubbock and Crosbyton

d down	P. & S. F. Ry.	Read up
Mls.	Table **86**	90 Ex.Su. Mixed
	Central Standard Time	PM
.0	Lv......Lubbock......Ar 10a, 79, 79a, 87,88	1.00
12.0	"......Idalou......Lv	12.24
20.3	"......Lorenzo......"	12.04
29.1	"......Ralls......"	11.42
38.5	Ar......Crosbyton......Lv	11.15
		AM

Lubbock and Bledsoe

d down	P. & S. F. Ry.	Read up
Mls.	Table **87**	80 Ex.Su. Mixed
	Central Standard Time	PM
.0	Lv......Lubbock......Ar 10a, 79, 79a, 86,88	3.10
7.0	"......Doud......Lv	f 2.28
13.0	"......Hurlwood......"	f 2.14
32.7	"......Levelland......"	1.28
46.2	"......Whiteface......"	12.57
57.5	"......Lehman......"	12.30
69.8	Ar........Bledsoe......Lv	12.01
		PM

Lubbock and Seagraves

d down	P. & S. F. Ry.	Read up
Mls.	Table **88**	78 Ex.Su. Mixed
	Central Standard Time	PM
.0	Lv......Lubbock......Ar 10a, 79,79a, 86, 87	3.00
7.0	"......Doud......Lv	f 2.18
23.2	"......Ropes......"	1.40
29.0	"......Meadow......"	1.25
40.8	"......Brownfield......"	12.58
64.0	Ar......Seagraves......Lv	12.01
		PM

Slaton and Lamesa

d down	P. & S. F. Ry.	Read up
Mls.	Table **89**	84 Ex.Su. Mixed
	Central Standard Time	PM
.0	Lv......Slaton 10a, 79a.... Ar	1.00
11.0	"......Wilson......Lv	12.30
22.3	"......Tahoka......"	12.05
37.1	"......O'Donnell......"	11.40
54.7	Ar......Lamesa......Lv	11.01
		AM

San Angelo and Sonora

d down	P. & S. F. Ry.	Read up
Mls.	Table **90**	128 Ex.Su. Mixed
	Central Standard Time	PM
.0	Lv. San Angelo 66, 67, 72.78 Ar	2.00
18.8	"......Christoval......Lv	f 1.20
44.7	"......Eldorado......"	12.30
66.4	Ar......Sonora......Lv	11.30
		AM

Santa Fe operated a fleet of mixed trains. Tables 84 through 90 of the Spring, 1960 timetable shows a group on the Panhandle and Santa Fe Railway with a variety of distances for as short as 26.6 miles and as long as 69.8 miles.

On the other hand, the M-122, built by Electro-Motive in 1929 was reconfigured with end platforms and assigned to switch engine duties. The M-122 is between assignments at Paris, Texas in August, 1959. (Harold K. Vollrath Collection)

Here is a prime example of a steam powered local in the early part of the streamline era, May 9, 1938. Train No. 14 is at Palmer Lake, Colorado with the 3510 for power and six cars. The train is charging forward to make up time despite the fact that it is several hours late. It was the connection with the Chief for the La Junta – Denver service. (Otto Perry, Denver Public Library, Western History Collection, OP 1642)

The main line locals were what one could call a "Pike Sized Passenger Train," meaning it was practically perfect for a model railroad layout - if not perfect! In this case, the San Bernardino Local is leaving Los Angeles in February, 1935 - a year ahead of the Streamlined Era. No. 41 operated to LA in the morning, and returned to San Bernardino later in the morning. In 1936, there were six passenger trains in each direction between LA and San Bernardino including the single pair of local trains 41 and 42. Now in 2004, there are 15 Metrolink commuter trains in each direction between Los Angeles and San Bernardino. (Harold K. Vollrath Collection)

Combine No. 2325 was also in mixed train service, and is bringing up the rear of such a train at Dodge City, Kansas in May, 1950. At that time, the car operated on trains 73 and 74 between Dodge City and Boise City on a Daily Except Saturday assignment for the 159.5 mile run. (Fred Springer, Harold K. Vollrath Collection)

Santa Fe Combine No. 2026 was a wooden car assigned to Mixed Train service. The car is between runs at Presidio, Texas for trains 129 and 130, which provided tri-weekly service between Presidio and San Angelo in 1955. (Fred Springer, Harold K. Vollrath Collection)

As we complete this chapter on branch line trains and local passenger services, it is getting close to the Amtrak Era in this May, 23, 1969 photo. In fact Amtrak is less than two years away. The Denver train connected with the Chief at La Junta. The two car train operated as train 191 departing Denver for Pueblo. At Pueblo, 191 became 190 for the remainder of the trip to La Junta. Returning, the train operated as 201 from La Junta to Pueblo and became 200 for the remainder of the run into Denver. The line between Denver and Pueblo was a joint operation over the Rio Grande, and therefore the trains were designated westbound to Pueblo with odd numbers, and eastbound into Denver with even numbers. South of Pueblo, the train was an eastbound run with an even number to La Junta, while the return run was westbound with an odd number. (William S. Kuba)

Chapter 5 - CALIFORNIA CORRIDOR SERVICES

The Santa Fe served two important areas in California for its entire career as a passenger carrier. The company operated a fleet of trains known as the San Diegans between Los Angeles and San Diego. Looking a bit north to Bakersfield, the railroad operated still another group known as the *Golden States* between Bakersfield and Oakland. The latter also included bus service connections between Los Angeles and Bakersfield as well as over the Bay between Oakland and San Francisco. These two corridors, as time progressed through the latter part of the Twentieth Century, would need even more passenger service. (Refer to Chapter 12 for the Amtrak Services on Santa Fe routes in California.) Let's take a look at the two corridors from the 1950s through to the implementation of Amtrak in May, 1971.

GOLDEN STATE ROUTE

The Golden State Route was (and is) a Los Angeles - San Francisco corridor via Bakersfield, Stockton and Oakland. During the early 1950s, the Santa Fe operated four trains in each direction on a daily basis. Two of the trains were *Golden States*, while the other two sets were different types of trains.

The *Golden State* schedules, trains 61 and 63, provided basic late morning and afternoon departures respectively from Bakersfield with 5 hour, 40 minute schedules to Oakland over the 314 mile distance. The southbound runs, trains 60 and 62, provided a morning run and an early evening run from Oakland to Bakerfield. No. 60 made the run in 5 hours, 55 minutes, while 62 did the run in 5 hours, 45 minutes. The *Golden States* were equipped with streamlined chair cars, chair lounge car and a lunch-counter dining car.

The other two sets of trains operating in the early 1950s consisted of an overnight run, trains 6 and 7, which provided coach service only. The trains also handled mail and express. The second set of trains was rather interesting. The train numbers were 23 and 4. No. 23 was an extension of the secondary train, the *Grand Canyon*, which provided quite an interesting type of service between Chicago and Oakland.

Westbound No. 23 handled a through sleeping car, 6 Section, 6 Roomette, and 4 Double Bedrooms to Bakersfield. At Bakersfield, the car was transferred to train 61 for completion of the run to Oakland. According to the time tables in 1953, train 23 departed Bakersfield at 10:45 a.m., 25 minutes before *Golden State*, No. 61's departure at 11:10. While 61 arrived at Oakland at 4:50 p.m., No. 23 did not arrive at Oakland until 7:10 p.m. No. 23 provided chair car service as well as a dining car.

The Oakland to Bakersfield trains were number 4 and 6. Train 4 was the *California Limited* with a departure 1 hour, 15 minutes after No. 60's departure at 8:10 a.m. Train 4 provided chair car service, a dining car and included a 10 section, 1 drawing room, 2 compartment sleeping car for its Oakland to Chicago run. As mentioned previously, overnight No. 6 provided chair car service only.

The picture began to change as time went on by 1957-58. At that time, there were still four passenger trains in each direction between Bakersfield and Oakland. The *Golden States* were still numbered 60, 61, 62 and 63. Trains 60 and 62 provided the morning and afternoon runs to Oakland, while 61 provided a late morning run and 63 a later afternoon departure from Oakland to Bakersfield. The trains still provided full chair car service, a lounge car and also a Fred Harvey lunch-counter dining car.

Meanwhile, the biggest change took place with the transcontinental train operations. The new train operation was the *San Francisco Chief*, trains 1 and 2. No. 1 provided an early morning departure from Bakersfield (running from Chicago), departing at 6:45 a.m. and arriving at Oakland at 1:05 p.m. No. 2 departed Oakland at 11:25 a.m. providing a mid-day schedule to Bakersfield for its run to Chicago. The *Chief* provided chair car and dining car service for the Bakersfield - Oakland passengers. The overnight trains were 6 and 7 with only the chair car for passengers.

More changes took place by the early 1960s. For example, in 1963, the Santa Fe operated three trains in each direction between Bakersfield and Richmond. The trains no longer operated through to Oakland. The *Golden State* train operations had been cut back to one train, No. 63 from Bakersfield to Richmond, but two *Golden States* continued to operate from Richmond to Bakersfield, Numbers 60 and 62. No. 63 departed Bakersfield at 1:45 p.m. with a 7:10 p.m. arrival at Richmond. The distance Bakersfield and Richmond was (is) 301 miles.

Trains 60 and 62 provided morning and evening services from Richmond to Bakersfield. No. 60 departed 7:30 a.m. with a 1:10 p.m. arrival, and 62 departed 6:00 p.m. with a 11:40 p.m. arrival time. The trains still carried a full lounge car and a Fred Harvey lunch-counter dining car on 60 and 63. The lounge car provided beverages and sandwiches on train 62. Essentially, the lunch-counter dining car had but a 25 minute turn from No. 60 to 63 at Richmond.

Trains 1, the *San Francisco Chief*, provided an early

Los Angeles to Bakersfield, Oakland and San Francisco

NORTH—Read down   SOUTH—Read up

Motor Coach Daily	Motor Coach Daily	Mls.	Table P	Motor Coach Daily		Motor Coach Daily
....	11.15AM	....	0	*(Pacific Standard Time)* Lv Los Angeles (Union Station) Ar	4.20PM	....	1.45AM
....	11.10AM			" .... Pasadena .... "	4.23PM	....
....	11.25AM	9		" .... Glendale .... "	4.02PM	....
....	11.40AM	13		" .... Burbank .... "	3.51PM	....
11.33AM	....			Lv .... Hollywood .... Ar	4.02PM	....	1.30AM
11.48AM	....			" .... N. Hollywood .... "	3.46PM	....	1.18AM
12.07PM	12.07PM	24		Lv .... San Fernando .... Ar	3.29PM	....	1.03AM
2.15PM	2.15PM	112		Ar Bakersfield (Santa Fe Sta.) Lv	1.20PM	....	11.10PM

No. 7 Daily	No. 63 Golden Gate Daily	No. 1 San Francisco Chief Daily	Mla.		No. 60 Golden Gate Daily	No. 2 San Francisco Chief Daily	No. 62 Golden Gate Daily
8.20PM	2.30PM	7.45AM	112	Lv .... Bakersfield .... Ar	1.10PM	5.25PM	10.59PM
10.55PM	4.30PM	9.45AM	222	" .... Fresno .... "	11.15AM	3.30PM	9.00PM
12.05AM	5.25PM	10.40AM	280	" .... Merced .... "	10.15AM	2.30PM	8.00PM
1.30AM	6.31PM	11.50AM	346	" .... Stockton .... "	9.10AM	1.24PM	6.52PM
3.15AM	7.55PM	1.30PM	414	Ar .... Richmond Lv	7.45AM	11.59AM	5.30PM

Motor Coach	Motor Coach	Motor Coach			Motor Coach	Motor Coach	Motor Coach
3.20AM	8.00PM	1.35PM	414	Lv .... Richmond .... Ar	7.40AM	11.55AM	5.25PM
3.45AM	8.25PM	2.00PM	423	" .... Berkeley .... "	7.15AM	11.30AM	5.00PM
3.55AM	8.35PM	2.10PM	426	" .... Oakland .... "	7.05AM	11.20AM	4.50PM
4.15AM	8.40PM	2.15PM	433	Ar San Francisco (P.S.T.) Lv	7.00AM	11.15AM	4.45PM

Equipment
GOLDEN GATE STREAMLINERS
Trains 60, 62 and 63

Lightweight streamlined trains operating daily between Bakersfield and Richmond. Air-conditioned, each train carries baggage and chair cars, full-lounge and Fred Harvey lunch-counter dining car. Motor Coaches are streamlined and air-conditioned.

Tables P and Q illustrate the California Corridor services in the Spring, 1960 Timetable including the frequency of the San Diegans during that period of time.

Los Angeles and San Diego

SOUTH—Read down   NORTH—Read up

80 San Diegan Daily	78 San Diegan Sundays and Holidays. Ø	76 San Diegan Daily	74 San Diegan Daily	72 San Diegan Daily	70 San Diegan Daily	Miles	Table Q	71 San Diegan Except Sundays and Holidays Ø	73 San Diegan Daily	75 San Diegan Daily	77 San Diegan Daily	79 San Diegan Daily	81 San Diegan Sundays and Holidays. Ø
11.45PM	7.30PM	4.45PM	1.30PM	9.30AM	6.45AM	0	Lv ... Los Angeles (P.S.T.) ... Ar	7.45AM	10.15AM	2.45PM	6.15PM	9.00PM	11.00PM
12.50AM	8.15PM	5.35PM	2.20PM	10.22AM	7.30AM	36	" .... Santa Ana Lv	6.47AM	1.39PM	5.18PM	4.25PM	7.58PM	10.10PM
2.00AM	9.05PM	6.25PM	3.10PM	11.14AM	8.23AM	87	" .... Oceanside .... "	6.02AM	8.25AM	12.49PM	4.25PM	7.05PM	9.20PM
3.00AM	10.00PM	7.30PM	4.15PM	12.15PM	9.30AM	128	Ar ... San Diego (P.S.T.) ... Lv	5.15AM	7.30AM	11.59AM	3.30PM	6.00PM	8.30PM

SAN DIEGAN STREAMLINERS (Air-conditioned)
Trains 70, 71, 72, 73, 74, 75, 76, 77, 78, 79, 80, 81

Club-lounge car and non-smoking car on San Diegans except train No. 80 and 81.

EXPLANATORY NOTES:

Sec.—Section; D. R.—Drawing Room; Comps.—Compartments; Obs.—Observation; D. B. R.—Double Bedroom. f Flag stop.
For explanation of Reference Marks see pages 14 and 15.

Ø Holidays referred to are Memorial Day, Fourth of July, Labor Day, Thanksgiving Day, Christmas Day, New Years Day and Washington's Birthday:

Time shown in light figures indicates a.m.   Time shown in dark figures indicates p.m.

---

morning departure from Bakersfield with a 12:45 p.m. arrival in Richmond; while No. 2 departed Richmond at 12:01 p.m. for Bakersfield. Train 7 from Bakersfield to Richmond was the only overnight service - one direction only. No. 6 had been discontinued.

The 1967 timetables listed two Santa Fe trains in each direction between Bakersfield and Richmond. One set was the *San Francisco Chief*, Numbers 1 and 2; while the other was simply listed as 7 and 8. The Chief, No. 1, continued to provide a morning run to Richmond, 8:00 a.m. with a 1:45 p.m. arrival, with No. 2 departing Richmond at 11:15 a.m. and arriving at Bakersfield at 4:35 p.m.

Train 7 departed Bakersfield at 7:35 p.m. with a 2:15 a.m. arrival in Richmond, while No. 8 departed Richmond at 6:30 p.m. with a 12:15 a.m. arrival in Bakersfield.

An interesting addition to the schedules was the listing of the Southern Pacific *San Joaquin Daylight*, trains 51 and 52, between Bakersfield and Richmond. No. 51 departed Bakersfield at 10:45 a.m. with a 4:55 p.m. arrival in Richmond; while No. 52 departed Richmond at 8:23 a.m. arriving at Bakersfield at 2:08 p.m. The SP trains operated to and from Oakland.

The Santa Fe continued to provide bus connections for the trains between Los Angeles and Bakersfield as well as between Richmond and San Francisco.

The *San Francisco Chief* was the only train operation for the Santa Fe in 1968 until Amtrak. The SP's *San Joaquin Daylight* was included in the time table.

THE SAN DIEGANS

The *San Diegans* were a set of streamlined trains that provided a substantial base line for train service between Los Angeles and San Diego, a distance of 128 miles. During the early 1950s, the Santa Fe operated seven trains in each direction between the two cities in this Southern California Corridor. Four of the trains were listed as *San Diegans*. What did the service look like with some rather interesting innovations in passenger service during the early 1950s? What the Santa Fe was doing in 1952 was incredible service wise, and in many ways, was a prologue to the Amtrak *Surfliners* in 2003.

May, 1952 was indeed a mile post in train operations on the Santa Fe's Los Angeles - San Diego "Surf Line" as it was referred to a half century ago. Additional operating profits and improved public and community relations were won by the railroad as a result of additional passenger services during that month. The new service consisted of two additional round trips (for a total 7 each way), one being a non-stop train operated with a single train consisting of two RDC-1s from the Budd Company. There were some interesting reasons as to why the Santa Fe added the trains, particularly with the Rail Diesel Cars.

There was a tremendous population growth in the LA and San Diego areas after 1946. The Santa Fe management decided that in order to improve the profitability of the Surf Line, additional trains would need to be added. It was a successful venture because between May, 1952 and the end of the year, passenger volume increased by 12 per cent. Furthermore, the company was very delighted over the fact that the relationship with the communities and the Santa Fe's reputation improved substantially.

One of the RDC round trips operated on a non-stop schedule of 2 hours, 15 minutes. This was an average speed of 57 miles per hour for the 128 mile run. The second RDC round trip made ten intermediate stops and achieved an average speed of 46 miles per hour. The Surf Line, by the way, was 100 mile an hour territory with Automatic Train Stop signal systems for all of the passenger trains including the RDC equipment.

The RDC trains were operated by five-man crews including the engineer, fireman, conductor, flagman and uniformed coach attendant. The coach seats were walk-over types with a high back and foam rubber headrest pad. Each car was divided with smoking and non-smoking sections. As a side note, the rail fares for the LA - San Diego Corridor averaged 1.8 cents per mile in 1952.

The consists of the *San Diegans* in 1953 were 8 car streamlined trains with an additional 3 extra coaches on week-ends. The trains were limited to 11 cars during that period of time. Motive power could consist of the two unit or four unit passenger F unit combinations, depending upon the length of the train. The schedules of the trains were designed for the best possible use for the traveling public on the Surf Line corridor. Let's take a closer look at some of the operations between 1953 and 1971.

The schedules of the *San Diegans* were spread throughout the day. Of the three trains that were not *San Diegans*, two were essentially local trains in each direction, numbers 75 and 83 northbound, and 70 and 80 southbound. What is interesting about No. 70 is that it was an overnight train from LA to San Diego. There was not a corresponding overnight run northbound. Train 80 was the southbound day time local.

Still another pair of non-*San Diegan* trains were No. 81 and 82, the RDCs. This pair of trains provided a non-stop run from San Diego in the morning (7:15 a.m.) with a 2 hour, 15 minute schedule. No. 82 provided the afternoon non-stop run in the late afternoon from LA to San Diego. No. 82 departed LA at 4:30 p.m.

The Non-*San Diegans*, train numbers 70, 75, 80, 81, 82, and 83 were equipped with chair cars only. All seats were reserved for the non-stop trains 81 and 82.

The *San Diegans* in 1953 were numbered 71, 72, 73, 74, 76, 77, 78, and 79. The trains were equipped with chair cars and a club-diner. The scheduled running times in 1953 ranged from 2 hours, 45 minutes to 2 hours, 50 minutes. The slowest of all trains was No. 70, the overnight from LA to San Diego with a schedule of 5 hours, 15 minutes. No. 70 departed LA at 11:30 p.m. and arrived in San Diego at 4:45 a.m.

All of the trains were designated *San Diegans* by the mid-1950s. Some of the trains operated on even faster schedules in 1957, such as No. 78, an evening train from LA to San Diego with schedule from 8:00 p.m. to 10:30 p.m. Train No. 80 continued to provide the overnight service from LA to San Diego, departing LA at 11:45 with a 3:00 a.m. arrival in San Diego. The number of trains between the early 1950s and the mid-1950s, for example 1957, was reduced by one each way with 6 San Diegans in each direction on a daily basis.

Ten of the 12 *San Diegans*, numbered consecutively from 70 to 81, were equipped with both chair cars and a club-lounge car. Snack service was available in the club-lounge. Trains 80, the overnight; and No. 81, the late evening train from San Diego to LA (8:00 p.m. to 10:30 p.m.) were assigned chair cars only. There were still six *San Diegans*, scheduled throughout the day, in each direction in 1963.

Table No. 6 from the Spring, 1960 timetable illustrates the coordinated bus services with the Golden Gates between Los Angeles and Bakersfield, and between Richmond and the San Francisco Bay area.

Between 1963 and 1967, three trains were discontinued in each direction leaving only three trains each way daily. The 1967 time table listed the Northbound trains 73, 75, and 77 departed San Diego at 7:00 a.m., 11:30 a.m., and 4:00 p.m., all with 2 hour, 55 minute schedules.

Southbound trains 74, 76, and 78 departed Los Angeles at 7:30 a.m., 11:00 a.m. and 7:45 p.m., again with 2 hour, 55 minute running times.

Four of the trains, 73, 76, 77 and 78 were equipped with a Lounge Car for beverages and light refreshments. Trains 74 and 75 did not carry baggage, remains or pets.

The final three trains per day basically continued until

Amtrak in May, 1971. The first Amtrak schedule listed two trains daily in each direction with a third train southbound on Tuesday, Friday and Sunday, and northbound on Sunday, Wednesday and Friday. As time went on, the frequency of trains would expand until 2003, with 11 trains each way Monday through Thursday, 12 each way on Friday, Saturday and Sunday. See Chapter 12 for the Amtrak Train Services on the Santa Fe.

Reserved seat accommodations with a moderate extra charge were provided on the *San Diegans* as well as trains 81 and 82, which provided a morning run to LA, and a late afternoon to San Diego respectively. Thus during the 1950s, passengers could obtain reserved seats on five trains in each direction. This photo shows one example of the types of seating with leg rests provided for the reserved seating. Truly, the Santa Fe was the way to go "all the way." (Santa Fe Railway Photo, Patrick C. Dorin Collection)

The Santa Fe's fleet of *San Diegans* serving the LA-San Diego Corridor provided the cornerstone for the future of passenger transportation services. The trains provided fast comfortable service with streamlined equipment including Chair Cars, Club Diner and a Baggage Car. In this publicity photo, a southbound San Diegan is arriving at the San Diego station. Throughout the 1940s and into the 1950s, the *San Diegans* were running with as many as 16 cars, which required the four units as shown in this photo. (Santa Fe Railway Photo, Harry Stegmaier Collection)

Motive power on the *San Diegans* included the Alco PAs as well as the Electro-Motive F units. A southbound *San Diegan* is climbing through Rose Canyon on its fast run from Los Angeles to San Diego. (Santa Fe Railway Photo, Kansas State Historical Society Collection)

Budd Rail Diesel Cars also served on the Los Angeles - San Diego Corridor as illustrated here with a two car set at San Diego in October, 1954. The two car train began service in the late spring of 1952. The RDCs operated provided two additional round trips daily on the Surf Line Corridor. The RDC-1s were numbered DC-191 and DC-192. The two car also operated one round trip as a non-stop run in 2 hours, 15 minutes, which was 30 minutes faster than a *San Diegan* schedule. The non-stop runs included No. 81 which departed San Diego at 7:15 a.m. with a 9:30 arrival in LA, while No. 82 departed LA at 4:30 p.m. for a 6:45 p.m. arrival in San Diego. The other round trip was a local run. It was an example of the versatility of the Rail Diesel Car. The DC-192 and 191 are laying over at the San Diego Depot between runs in October, 1954. (Collection of Harold K. Vollrath)

The *Golden Gates* were the Santa Fe streamliners between Bakersfield and the San Francisco Bay area. A westbound *Golden Gate* has just arrived at Oakland during its early career (when the trains arrived and departed Oakland) and is meeting the bus to take the passengers over the Golden Gate Bridge to San Francisco. The Santa Fe was a pioneer with intermodal passenger services with their connecting bus services to and from the San Francisco. (Santa Fe Railway Photo, Kansas State Historical Society Collection)

This Santa Fe publicity photo illustrates one example of the superb *San Diegan* fleet. This northbound train consist of over a dozen cars including an Observation car as it races along the beautiful Pacific Coast toward LA. Note the coach ahead of the Observation Car is the Pendulum Coach. When this photo was taken in March, 1952, the Santa Fe operated 4 San Diegans in each direction between LA and San Diego as well three additional trains without the name. (Santa Fe Railway Photo, Kansas State Historical Society Collection)

TRAIN 60
OAKLAND – BAKERSFIELD

```
1 Baggage-Chair   Oakland – Bakersfield )
3 Chairs             "     –     "      )Monday to Thursday
1 LCD                "     –     "      )inclusive
1 Lounge             "     –     "      )2 extras
1 Chair              "     –     "      )Fri-Sat-Sun.
1 Chair-Obs.         "     –     "      )

          8 cars Oakland to Bakersfield (Mon-Tues-Wed-Thurs.)
         10   "      "    "      "       (Fri-Sat-Sun.)
```

TRAIN 61
BAKERSFIELD – OAKLAND

```
1 Baggage-Chair   Bakersfield – Oakland )
3 Chairs             "      –     "     )Monday to Thursday
1 LCD                "      –     "     )inclusive
1 Lounge             "      –     "     )2 extra chairs
1 Chair              "      –     "     )Fri-Sat-Sun.
1 Chair-Obs.         "      –     "     )

          8 cars Bakersfield to Oakland (Mon-Tues-Wed-Thurs.)
         10   "       "      "     "    (Fri-Sat-Sun.)
```

TRAIN 62
OAKLAND – BAKERSFIELD

```
1 30-40' Combn. (LW) Oakland – Barstow, Daily (For No. 8)
1 Baggage-Chair (or Bage) Oakland – Bakersfield, Daily
3 Chairs             Oakland – Bakersfield )Monday to Thursday
1 LCD                   "    –     "        )inclusive
1 Lounge                "    –     "        )2 extra chairs
1 Chair-Obs.            "    –     "        )Fri-Sat-Sun.

          8 cars Oakland to Bakersfield (Mon-Tues-Wed-Thurs.)
         10   "      "    "      "       (Fri-Sat-Sun.)
```

TRAIN 63
BAKERSFIELD – OAKLAND

```
1 30-40' Combn. (LW) Bakersfield – Oakland, Daily
1 Baggage-Chair         "       –    "    ,
3 Chairs                "       –    "     )Monday to Thursday
1 LCD                   "       –    "     )inclusive
1 Lounge                "       –    "     )2 extra chairs
1 Chair-Obs.            "       –    "     )Fri-Sat-Sun.

          8 cars Bakersfield to Oakland (Mon-Tues-Wed-Thurs.)
         10   "       "      "     "    (Fri-Sat-Sun.)
```

It is the year 1957, and this consist sheet shows the equipment operated on the Oakland – Bakersfield trains. Note the differences in the consists for the various days of the week. Week-end consists, including Friday, expanded to 10 cars. (Santa Fe Passenger Consist, 1957)

LOS ANGELES-SAN DIEGO

Southbound

Train 74	4 CC Mon-Fri 5 CC Sat 4 CC Sun
Train 76	4 CC Mon-Thur 5 CC Fri-Sun 1 Lounge 1 Bag
Train 78	4 CC Mon-Thur 6 CC Fri 5 CC Sun 1 Lounge 1 Bag

Northbound

Train 73	4 CC Mon-Fri 5 CC Sat 4 CC Sun 1 Lounge 1 BE
Train 75	3 CC
Train 77	5 CC Mon-Thur 7 CC Fri 5 CC Sat 7 CC Sun 1 Lounge 1 BE

The 1966 *San Diegan* consists were slimming down as time went by. The consists would vary according to weekdays or weekends. The longest train was No. 77 with seven cars, while the shortest was No. 75 with but 3 Chair Cars.

Chapter 6 - DINING AND LOUNGE CAR SERVICES

The Santa Fe operated a wide range of dining, lunch counter, cafe and lounge cars on many trains throughout its system. Overnight, transcontinental and many shorter runs were equipped with food and beverage service cars. Part of the Santa Fe's philosophy in providing food and beverage service was to provide passengers good reasons to be repeat travelers. One of the many things that made Santa Fe food and beverage services unique was the Fred Harvey services.

Fred Harvey was operating a group of hotels with restaurants throughout the mid-west in the 1870s. He had a number of ideas about how to expand and market his food services. One of which was to provide such services in railroad stations. The Santa Fe liked the idea, and brought in Fred Harvey to establish restaurant facilities in many depots. The food service was so delightful and successful that the Santa Fe decided to have Fred Harvey manage the company's Dining Car Operations.

The time tables listed dining car as Fred Harvey service throughout the history of the Santa Fe passenger services. Even with the decline in passenger services throughout North America in the 1950s, the Santa Fe was still operating 96 dining car crews across the system. Over 800 people were employed within the Fred Harvey Dining Car Services alone during the 1960s.

The Fred Harvey services provided a wide range of meals in the dining and lunch-counter cars. Breakfast, lunch and dinner were a delight, and according to one repeat passenger this writer knew in high school, it was one of the reasons he continued to ride the Santa Fe from Chicago to Kansas City. Dining and lounge car services added one more element to the comfort of train travel.

There were many interesting meals on the Santa Fe. One example was the new Champagne Dinner on the *Super Chief* in 1963. A complimentary service of champagne was served with variety of entrees of prime ribs, broiled lobster tails, breast of chicken continental or a London mixed grill.

The Santa Fe came up with some interesting innovations in the early 1960s to continue the positive meal service programs. One was an Automatic Food and Drink program. This concept became part of the Vendo-Lounge, one of the Santa Fe's latest edition to the passenger car fleet. The Vendo-Lounge was operated to supplement regular dining car service on the *Golden Gates* between Bakersfield and Richmon. Still other plans were to include it with other train services and operations.

Four vending machines were placed on each side of an aisle at the vestibule end the reconfigured lounge car. The various vending machines provided as follows:

* Cold food, sandwiches, waffles, salads, fruits and pie.
* Ice Cream bars.
* Coffee with or without cream and sugar, hot chocolate and bouillon.
* Cold drinks, both carbonated and non-carbonated with an ice dispenser.
* Nine selections of hot canned foods including soup and stews.
* Pastry, cakes, sweet rolls and dry cereals.
* Milk, chocolate milk and lemonade.
* Mints, gum, candy bars and cookies.

The Santa Fe Dining Car services were provided by Fred Harvey. The dining rooms were top quali can be observed with this photo of the interior of a Dining Car assigned to the *Super Chief*. (Sant Railway Photo, Harry Stegmaier Collection)

The various prices during the 1960s ranged from a dime (such as for doughnuts) to 50 cents for a meal of two waffles with butter and maple syrup. The car was operated by two attendants with one at the bar section, with the other at the vending machines. The machines were replenished en route if it was necessary. A refrigerator was also part of the equipment for supplies. Tables and chairs in the lounge section provided seating for 35 passengers. Thirty of which could be seated at the tables.

The Santa Fe had experimented with passenger cars equipped with vending machines during the 1950s. For example, a chair car operated on the Albuquerque - El Paso runs had been equipped with such food service. In this case, the machines provided hot and cold drinks as well as sandwiches.

Examples of Fred Harvey Dining Car Assignments

Early 1950s

Train	Equipment
Super Chief	Dining Car
The Chief	Dining Car and Cafe-Parlor Ash Fork to Phoenix
El Capitan	Two Lunch-Counter Diners
The Grand Canyon	Dining Car
	Cafe Observation Car La Junta to Denver
	Dining Cars on various sections, such as the Antelope
The Scout	Dining Car
California Limited	Dining Car
Kansas City Chief	Lunch-Counter Diner
The Kansas Cityan	Dining Car
Texas Chief	Lunch-Counter Diner
Chicagoan	Dining Car
Golden Gates	Lunch-Counter Dining Cars
San Diegans	Club-Diner
The Tulsan	Dining Car and Cafe Lounge over part of the route
The Oil Flyer	Dining Car or Diner-Lounge Car
California Special	Dining Car
Texan	Dining Car

The above assignments varied from train to train and within various sections of the trains over different routes.

1968

Train	Equipment
Super Chief	Dining Car
El Capitan	Hi-level Dining Car
San Francisco Chief	Dining Car
The Chief	Dining Car

Train	Equipment
The Texas Chief	Dining Car
Kansas Cityan	Lunch Counter-Dining Car
Chicagoan	Lunch Counter-Dining Car
Kansas City Chief	Dining Car
The Tulsan	Coffee-sandwich cart service

As described in Chapter 1, the number of trains had declined by the end of the 1960s as well as the wide variety of dining car assignments on the various trains.

Dinner is being served on the Dining Car assigned to the *Chief*. Passengers are being seated with comfortable seating and appropriately sized tables with adequate room for any type of meal. The 2 and 4 seating permitted passengers to have greater options regarding their seating with family and friends. It is interesting to note that many people have had the opportunity to meet new friends while eating in the Dining Car. One passenger told this writer that he met his future wife on the *Chief*. Also note the Native American Art as part of the super decor for the interior of the dining room. (Santa Fe Railway Photo, Harry Stegmaier Collection)

The full Dining Cars were not the only areas for meals. The Turquoise Room of the Santa Fe's *Super Chief* was a delight for a wide variety of passenger-gourmet dinners. The Turquoise Room was one of the first private dining rooms to be offered for passengers and small groups on any North American railroad. The Turquoise Room was located below the Pleasure Dome car assigned to the *Super Chief*. (Santa Fe Railway Photo, Harry Stegmaier Collection)

During the 1960s, the Santa Fe operated Automat Dining Cars on the *Golden State* between Bakersfield and Richmond. Part of the Automat Serving Section is to the left of the photo. Seating was designed for 2 and 4 passenger arrangements with triangular tables for two, and diamond shape tables for four. (Santa Fe Railway Photo, Kansas State Historical Society Collection)

The Santa Fe invested in a number of Lunch Counter Dining Cars for the *El Capitan* as well as for service on other routes. The dining room consisted of table seating for four passengers per table as well as the lunch counter which is in the background of the photo. (Santa Fe Railway Photo, Kansas State Historical Society Collection)

The Big Dome Lounge Cars provided two types of seating on the upper level. One section included table seating for enjoying snacks and beverages, while the main section provided seating similar to coach accommodations for observing the passing scenary.

The Big Dome Lounge cars operated on several trains including the *San Francisco Chief*. (Santa Fe Railway Photo, Patrick C. Dorin Collection)

The *El Capitan* Hi-Level Lounge Cars were equipped with a variety of seating and table accommodations for visiting, conversation and enjoying the passing scenery. This photo shows the differences with the Hi-Level cars compared to the conventional streamlined equipment from the inside out. (Santa Fe Railway Photo, Patrick C. Dorin Collection)

Santa Fe

Fred Harvey Food Service

Santa Fe offers you famous Fred Harvey Service in dining cars, hotels and dining stations

Dining car service on The Super Chief (trains 17 and 18) is a la carte. In addition to lunch-counter diner on The Chief (trains 19 and 20) there is a full length diner serving a la carte meals. Table d'hote dinners also are served on these trains.

Table d'hote meals (in addition to a la carte service) are served on the following trains, breakfast $1.20 and up; luncheon a la carte; dinner $2.20 and up.

NUMBER	TRAINS	BETWEEN
1-102 and 13-130		La Junta and Denver
23 and 4		Barstow and Oakland
11 and 12, The Kansas Cityan and		
The Chicagoan		Chicago and Oklahoma City
15 and 16, The Texas Chief		Chicago and Galveston
23 and 24, and 123 and 124, The Grand Canyon		Chicago, Los Angeles and Oakland
42 and 47		Ash Fork and Phoenix
47 and 48, The Oil Flyer		Kansas City and Tulsa
42-170 and 181-47		Phoenix and Wickenburg
211 and 212, The Tulsan		Kansas City and Tulsa

Table d'hote breakfast, $1.20 and up; a la carte luncheon and, or dinner served on the following trains: 5 and 6 between Kansas City and Ft. Worth; 9 and 10 The Kansas City Chief between Chicago and Kansas City.

EL CAPITAN (trains 21 and 22) and Lunch-Counter diner on THE CHIEF (trains 19 and 20), between Chicago and Los Angeles, Club Breakfast 65¢; Luncheon 85¢; Dinner $1.00. Special Club Steak dinner $2.45. Also a la carte service for all meals.

The SAN DIEGAN (trains 71, 72, 73, 74, 76 and 77) between Los Angeles and San Diego. Breakfast 95¢; Luncheon and Dinner, "Chefs Special" $1.50, also a la carte service for all meals.

THE GOLDEN GATE (trains 60, 61, 62 and 63) Breakfast 95¢ and $1.40; Luncheon a la carte; Dinner "Chefs Suggestion" $1.65; Table d'hote from $2.05. Also a la carte service for all meals.

California Limited (trains 3 and 4) between Wellington and Gallup: Table d'hote breakfast $1.40; dinner $2.15; also a la carte service for all meals. No dining car between Chicago and Wellington and Gallup and Los Angeles. Meals are served at dining stations.

Trains 66-75 and 76-65 between Houston and Clovis, Club Breakfast 70¢ and $1.00; Luncheon, "Chef's Suggestion and Special Lunch" $1.00; Dinner, "Chef's Suggestion" $1.50 and "Special" $2.45. Also a la carte service.

All dining cars serve special meals for children at substantially lower prices than for adults. All dining cars are air-conditioned.

FRED HARVEY HOTELS, RESTAURANTS AND DINING STATIONS

Fred Harvey dining stations—with counter or table service, or both—are located in or near several of the passenger depots. These dining stations offer table d'hote service, breakfast $1.15, luncheon $1.45, and dinner $1.65 up; also a la carte service at reasonable prices. Special children's meals at reduced prices.

Restaurants and lunch rooms in union terminals at Chicago, Kansas City, and Los Angeles are also under Fred Harvey management, offering meal service at moderate prices.

The station hotels are conveniently located for business and sight-seeing. Rates (European Plan) for one person range from $3.00 per day up for rooms without bath and from $4.00 per day up for rooms with bath.

RAND McNALLY & COMPANY, CHICAGO Issued January 10, 1954

Hotels, Restaurants and Dining Rooms

		Lunch Room	Dining Room	Guest Rooms
ARIZONA	El Tovar Hotel Grand Canyon		250	81
	Bright Angel Lodge Grand Canyon	225		98
	Fray Marcos Hotel Williams	53	68	22
	La Posada Hotel Winslow	116	72	70
CALIFORNIA	Union Station Los Angeles	80	285	
ILLINOIS	Dearborn Station Chicago	31	102	
KANSAS	Newton	115		
MISSOURI	Union Station Kansas City	300	145	
NEW MEXICO	Alvarado Hotel Albuquerque	116	135	118
	El Navajo Hotel Gallup	93	120	70
	La Fonda Hotel Santa Fe		350	216

PILLOW SERVICE

As a convenience to chair car passengers, pillows may be rented from NEWS AGENTS on all principal trains.

On trains 21 and 22, El Capitan, and 19 and 20, The Chief, the charge is 35¢ for the entire trip. On all other trains the charge is 25¢ per night.

PRINTED IN U.S.A.

The Santa Fe provided a substantial amount of information about the dining car service as well as the other services provided by Fred Harvey on the back page of the January, 1954 timetable. They listed all of the trains with such services plus the list of Fred Harvey Hotels, Restaurants and Dining Stations throughout the System. Yes, indeed, the Fred Harvey Food Service was another example of coordinated work systems – the team approach with many positive benefits.

Chapter 7 - MAIL AND EXPRESS SERVICES

The Santa Fe, as with all of the North American passenger services, handled a substantial amount of mail and express. The company operated a dedicated mail train between Chicago and California, No. 7 and 8, on a daily basis.

Virtually all of the Santa Fe passenger trains, with the exception of some locals, handled a Rail Post Office car with 15, 30 or 60 feet of mail space for sorting and other postal work to be done en route. The railroad operated an extensive fleet of both streamlined and heavy weight cars for the head-end business. This included full RPO cars, and combination RPO-Baggage equipment, as well as a wide variety of full Baggage cars. Still other equipment included 50 foot express box cars with high speed trucks. The wide diversity of equipment made the Santa Fe passenger trains even more interesting with some interesting challenges for modeling the trains.

Some major adjustments for handling mail on the Santa Fe took place in early 1961. In April of that year, the railroad and the Post Office Department began an experimental movement of containerized mail in passenger trains between Kansas City and the San Francisco Bay Area. Initially two types of equipment were tested. First was the 79 foot flat car with six wheel, roller bearing trucks with special equipment for handling containers. The second type was a Flexi-Van flat car, similar if not identical to the New York Central and Milwaukee Road equipment in the same type of service. Regular Flexi-Van containers operated on the Flexi-Van cars. The containers for the 79 foot flat were 8 by 8 by 19 foot boxes built by the Brown Trailer Company.

The first experimental run with a 79 foot flat car departed Kansas City on April 26 in the consist of the *San Francisco Chief*. The car arrived in Richmond, California in the early afternoon of April 28th. The Flexi-Van car was tested later in the week with the same type of schedule on the *San Francisco Chief*. The empty cars and containers returned to Kansas City on trains 62 and the Fast Mail No. 8. The containers operated on different days initially in order to conduct tests under the wide variety of mail volumes on different days of the week. The container cars were placed on the head-end of the *San Francisco Chief*.

The containers were routed from Kansas City to four Bay Area U.S. Mail distribution points: Oakland Terminal, West Oakland Terminal, San Francisco's Rincon Annex or the Ferry Annex Post Office. The containers were unloaded by fork lift trucks and placed on flat bed trucks for delivery to the Oakland and San Francisco post office receiving points. Further test runs were made between Kansas City and Los Angeles during the fall of 1961. The tests were successful, which in turn led to a full service operation for the Santa Fe's mail traffic.

The containerized mail traffic services were expanded in June, 1962. At that time a new daily service began with mail from Chicago and Kansas City to the San Francisco Bay area. The Santa Fe purchased 100 of the 8 by 8 by 20 foot containers and 25 specially-equipped flat cars capable of handling four containers each. The containers were painted silver with Santa Fe lettering at the top, and U.S. Mail as part of the lettering and container identifications.

The mail had been presorted at Chicago and Kansas City for the four Bay area terminals. The loaded containers continued to roll on the *San Francisco Chief*. As time went on, the company expanded the services with the U.S. Postal Service, which eventually led to still other operations with mail on the intermodal trains.

This chapter reviews some of the different types of head-end passenger equipment as well the types of services the various cars provided for the U.S. Mail, Railway Express, and passenger luggage.

The Santa Fe's Fast Mail between Chicago and California was numbered 7 and 8. No. 7 is shown arriving at Barstow, California during the days of steam with an incredible long train. The fourth car in the consist is a 60 foot Rail Post Office Car, which sorted mail all the way from Chicago to Los Angeles. (Santa Fe Railway Photo, Kansas State Historical Society Collection)

The *Fast Mail* is shown here at Dodge City, Kansas powered by 4 units with a mixture of heavyweight and streamlined baggage cars, box express cars as well as the all important Railway Post Office equipment. Trains 7 and 8 were designated as the "Fast Mail and Express" in the Division time tables. (William S. Kuba, June 9, 1963)

Mail and express traffic was handled on practically all Santa Fe passenger trains. By the mid-1960s, containers for mail traffic were also being handled on flat cars equipped with high speed trucks and steam lines for passenger train operation. This mid-1960s photo shows train No. 8 getting ready to depart Richmond, California for Bakersfield. By this time, according to a 1966 time table, the name Golden Gate was dropped. Thus No. 8 is not only providing an evening trip for coach passengers in the *Golden Gate* Corridor, but is also handling nine cars for mail and express. As a side note, No. 8 had been designated as a *Golden Gate* for a short period of time after train 62 had been discontinued and the train combined with the mail train No. 8. (Richard Steinheimer, Patrick Dorin Collection)

Mail and express was handled on nearly all of the Santa Fe passenger trains. This photo shows the *Super Chief* at Albuquerque, New Mexico with mail being loaded and unloaded from the RPO car, as well as to and from the baggage car which is also handling express and checked luggage. Note the wagons of mail bags to the left to the photo. (Santa Fe Railway Photo, John Sward)

TRAIN 7, CHICAGO TO KANSAS CITY

1	Express	New York-Kansas City, Ex. Mon)
1/3	Express	New York-Los Angeles, Ex. Mon-Tue)
1/3	Express	New York-Los Angeles, Ex. Mon) From
1/3	Express	New York-Los Angeles, Extra) NYC
1	Express	New York-Barstow, Wed-Thur-Fri-Sat)
1	Stge Mail	New York-Kansas City, Extra)
1/2	Stge Mail	Chicago-Los Angeles, Extra
1/2	Stge Mail	Chicago-Kansas City, Extra
1	Stge Mail	Chicago-Kansas City-San Diego, Daily (For 123)
1	60-Ft. RPO	Chicago-Kansas City, Ex. Sunday
2	60-Ft. RPO	Chicago-Kansas City, Daily
1	Stge Mail	Chicago-Los Angeles (Pouch) Daily
1	Stge Mail	Chicago-Los Angeles (Rotary) Daily
1	COF Car(Stge Mail)	Chicago-Richmond, Extra
1	Stge Mail	Chicago-Richmond (Local) Daily
1	Express	Chicago-Richmond, Daily
1	Ex. Messgr.	Chicago-Los Angeles, Daily
1	P. Box Exp.	Chicago-Los Angeles, Ex. Sun-Mon
1	Exp.-Rider	Chicago-Los Angeles, Daily
1	Express	Chicago-Streator, Sunday

TRAIN 7, KANSAS CITY TO LOS ANGELES

(Extra California carloads of mail and express in this position)

1/3	Express	New York-Los Angeles (Work LaJunta) Ex. Tue
1/2	Stge Mail	Chicago-Los Angeles, Extra
1	Express	New York-Barstow, Thur-Fri-Sat-Sun
1	Stge Mail	Kansas City-Albuquerque, Daily
1	Stge Mail	Kansas City-Los Angeles (open) Daily
1	60-Ft. RPO	Kansas City-Los Angeles, Daily
1	Stge Mail	Chicago-Los Angeles (Pouch) Daily
1	Stge Mail	Chicago-Los Angeles (Rotary) Daily
1	COF Car(Stge Mail)	Chicago/Kansas City-Richmond, Extra)
1	Stge Mail	Chicago-Richmond (Local) Daily) For
1	Stge Mail	Kansas City-Richmond (Local) Daily) North 7
1	Express	Kansas City-Richmond (Local) Daily) Barstow
1	Express	Chicago-Richmond, Daily)
1	Exp. Messgr.	Chicago-Los Angeles, Daily
1	Exp. (P. Box)	Chicago-Los Angeles, Ex. Mon-Tue.
1	Express-Rider	Chicago-Los Angeles, Daily

(Cars off Train 3 Gallup added to rear)

The *Fast Mail and Express*, trains 7 and 8, often exceeded 25 cars in length. This 1966 passenger consist sheet shows No. 7 between Chicago and Kansas City, and Kansas City and Los Angeles. Note how some of the car assignments operated only on certain days of the week. It is interesting that there were three 60 foot Rail Post Office cars between Chicago and Kansas City, while there was but one between Kansas City and Los Angeles. The 1966 consists included both express box cars as well as container cars. (Santa Fe Passenger Consist, 1966)

It is 1950 and the mail and express traffic is as busy as ever. This photo from Otto Perry shows the *Fast Mail and Express* west of Florence, Kansas with 16 cars on a bright summer day on July 1, 1950. (Denver Public Library, Western History Collection, OP2177)

Chapter 8 - PASSENGER SPECIALS, BUSINESS CARS and the SUPER C

The Santa Fe operated a wide variety of special passenger trains including Business Car Specials, and with Business Cars as part of the consist of freight trains. The latter was especially true on freight only routes and especially after the advent of Amtrak. Since the Business Cars played a special role, they are included in this chapter of specials. The *Super C* is also included because it is prime example of how Business Cars were part of the consist of freight trains, especially with new innovations in scheduling and services. The chapter is divided into three sections including Passenger Specials, Business Cars and Trains, and the *Super C* with its roots from the *Super Chief*.

PASSENGER SPECIALS

The Santa Fe was truly a prominent passenger orientated railroad in North America for many decades. As a result of their positive philosophy of working with and for the traveling public, the Santa Fe attracted a fairly large number of special requests for passenger trains. This included Boy and Girl Scout Specials, Athletic events, Groups such as the Shriners, and Military Troop Specials, and the list can go on and on.

Passenger Specials operated as either "Passenger Extras" with white flags on the engine indicating an extra, non-scheduled train; or sometimes as a second or even third section of a scheduled passenger train. The consist of the trains could vary with combinations of heavy weight and streamlined equipment, passenger equipment from many other railroads, and train lengths varying from relatively short - such as 4 or 5 cars, to well over 20 - sometimes over 25 cars. Color schemes could also vary. For example, Pullman cars with colors from almost a dozen railroads could be found in a special. Furthermore, since the Santa Fe had at least four colors: silver, dark or Pullman green, two-tone grey and a full grey paint application; the diversity of colors extended even more.

The Santa Fe also operated a number of rail-fan specials over the years including steam powered trains. The Santa Fe owned and operated one steam locomotive, the 4-8-4 No. 3751, which was built by Baldwin in 1941. Unfortunately, the 3751 is no longer on the BN&SF roster. Finally, with Amtrak, the number of specials has declined but it can still happen on the Santa Fe. Business Car trains also fall into the category of special trains.

The Santa Fe merger with the Burlington Northern produced an even larger fleet of passenger equipment for special runs. Former commuter cars were rebuilt for special operations on the railroad, and now carry the full name Burlington Northern & Santa Fe in the letter board with the silver color scheme. And finally, some of this equipment has actually been powered by the Milwaukee Road 4-8-4 No. 261 steam locomotive. Special steam runs on the AT&SF, and later the BN&SF, have a history of a variety of power from various areas.

Special passenger runs bring back many memories for many people, both the passengers and the audiences on track side as the train rolls by. The specials provide people a chance to relax and get to know each other at deeper levels, and thus can enjoy the convention, rail fan special, or many other activities even more.

It can be said that this is the ultimate with passenger specials headed up by a mixture of steam power and modern diesel locomotives. It is September 8, 1992, and the restored 4-8-4 Northern, No. 3751 is at Kansas City, Missouri with a "Passenger Extra" with a variety of equipment including Baggage Cars, Chair Cars and a Big Dome Lounge Car.

The train is gaining speed as the 3751 smokes it up a romance and beauty of railroading second to none. It brings a combination of history with railroading today, and a way to show what railroading is all about. (Harold K. Vollrath Collection)

ing up a bit in history, this photo shows an eastbound troop train in November, ... The consist of 19 cars included five head-end cars for supplies and other ...ment for the troops onboard. The train is eastbound at Robinson, New ...co. (Otto Perry, Denver Public Library, Western History Collection, OP1949)

Mountaineer	85' 0"	Pullman, 1949
Atchison	85' 0"	Pullman, 1949
Topeka	87' 6"	Budd, 1957
Santa Fe	87' 6"	Budd, 1957

This of course is not the full story of the Business Car fleet, which included some 60 foot, wood cars with steel underframes as late as the 1960s, 401 to 408 and 423, 424, 426, and 428. Five other all steel cars were numbered 9, 17, 20, 21, and 22.

In addition to the Business Cars, the Santa Fe also maintained passenger equipment for instruction, test equipment, simulator classroom cars in the 1960s as follows:

Type	Number	Length	Type of	Builder/Date
Instruction	5000	84' 0"	6 Wheel	Pullman, 1926
Test Car	5015	80' 3"	6 Wheel	Pullman, 1914
Repair Cars	5031	78' 3"	6 Wheel	Pullman, 1910
	5032	70' 0"	6 Wheel	Pullman, 1914
Simulator	5008	85' 0"	4 Wheel	Santa Fe, 1969
Cars	5009	82' 0"	6 Wheel	Santa Fe, 1970
Track	85		6 Wheel	
Geometry	86		4 Wheel	Support Car
Cars				

This equipment could also be observed operating in passenger trains or in the Business Car Specials. It all depended upon the purpose of the trip.

THE SUPER C AND ITS ROOTS FROM THE SUPER CHIEF

What is this? One might ask! A section of freight service in a passenger train and equipment book. In this case, it is important because the Super C Intermodal Train literally had its operating roots in the fast operations of the Super Chief. It is an example of how concepts utilized with a passenger train operation could be implemented for a fast, time driven, priority freight service - The Super C Intermodal between Chicago and Los Angeles.

The idea for the Super C was conceived with substantial planning in 1967. It was to be an intermodal train running on basically a 40 hour schedule. The consist was limited to trailers and containers - TOFC/COFC with an initial 15 to 20 car maximum. The first run of the Super C took place on January 17, 1968. The consist included a Pullman sleeping car and two Business Cars, which were occupied by the Santa Fe President John S. Reed, Operating Vice President R. D. Shelton, Traffic Vice President T. M. Caiazza and several newsmen. It was not only the first run, but also a celebration for launching a new train service that would also be handling U.S. Mail. The first trip from Chicago to Los Angeles took only 35 hours. How about that? That was faster than the Super Chief. The train was powered by two brand new Electro-Motive 3600 horsepower FP45s.

The Super C began to handle mail in May, 1969. The train was designated to handle 15 to 20 vans daily in each

BUSINESS CARS AND TRAINS

The Santa Fe owned and operated a fleet of Business Cars for a variety of reasons including inspection trips, board of directors' specials and tours for shippers as well as other groups and organizations. Sometimes the cars were operated on special trains with revenue passengers. With the observation platforms at the rear of the car, the Business Cars added an artistic touch to the rear of any train.

The Business Cars could operate on the rear of a regular passenger train, or a group of cars could be part of a special which may have included Sleeping Cars, Chair Cars and Dining and Lounge Cars. There was no limit to the types of trains Business Car could be observed bringing up the rear, and this included freight and intermodal trains as well. The Super C, by the way, was a typical example of a train which might have included a Business Car.

During the last few decades of Santa Fe operations, including into the Burlington Northern and Santa Fe era, the Business Car equipment has been painted in the traditional Santa Fe silver colors. What did the fleet consist of prior to Amtrak?

Roster During the 1960s

Car Numbers/Names	Length	Remarks, Builder and Year
Heavyweight Equipment		
31	82' 6"	Pullman, 1918
32	82' 1"	Pullman, 1923
34	82' 6"	Pullman, 1923
35	83' 7"	Pullman, 1923
36	82' 8"	Pullman, 1924
38	81' 11"	Pullman, 1925
39	83' 6"	Pullman, 1928
Lightweight Equipment		

This passenger extra was part of an American Express Banner Tour, and is shown here arriving at Los Angeles on this August 1, 1940 day with 13 cars. (Otto Perry, Denver Public Library, Western History Collection, OP 1910)

The Pacific 3433 is heading a Football Special at Dallas, Texas with an 8 car consist on January 1, 1938. Football Specials were operated for both Professional and University Football Games, and in a few rare instances still happens in the 21st Century. However in the 1920s and 30s, High School teams and fans also traveled on Football Specials. It is interesting to note that in those days, the High School players traveled in Pullman cars with the football coach in the Drawing Room. The School Principal traveled in the Chair car. (Otto Perry, Denver Public Library, Western History Collection, OP 1487)

direction. The Westbound *Super C* carried mail for Kansas City and LA from Chicago as well as from seven eastern cities: New York, Boston, Springfield, Harrisburg, Philadelphia, Cleveland and Detroit. The eastbound operation carried mail from Los Angeles and Kansas City to Chicago and the points east. It is interesting to note that the *Super C's* 40 hour schedule was often exceeded. The train averaged 37 hours for its run between Chicago and Los Angeles.

Mail and express were (and are with Amtrak) a crucial element in the total passenger services. And so one could say, with a bit of stretched imagination of course, that the Super C ultimately became part of the passenger fleet. Especially with the use of FP45s for power, which were painted in the red and silver scheme common for all passenger motive power.

As a final note - as a sidebar, Amtrak's *Southwest Chief* - over the Santa Fe from Chicago to Los Angeles - handled intermodal equipment - RoadRailers. In a sense, the Super C and the passenger trains merged together - again stretching the imagination!

Business Car No. 9 was part of the series within the numbers 4 to 15. No. 9 was photographed in service on an Inspection Trip at Topeka, Kansas in October, 1950. (Harold K. Vollrath Collection)

Below: The Santa Fe operated a fleet of Division Superintendent's Business Cars. Two such cars, numbers 408 and 409 were built by Pullman in November, 1929 as illustrated in this photo. For the most part, this group of cars were painted in the Pullman Green Scheme. (Santa Fe Railway, Kansas State Historical Society Collection)

Superintendent's Business Car No. 405's portrait was taken in March, 1949 at Dodge City, Kansas. Note the 4 wheel trucks for this group of 60 foot cars. (Harold K. Vollrath Collection)

Business Car No. 20 was a full length heavyweight car that eventually acquired the silver paint scheme. The 20 is shown here at Chicago in September, 1967. The car operated system wide for many types of inspection trips as well as for shippers. (Owen Leander, J. Michael Gruber Collection)

Still another important part of the Santa Fe passenger car fleet were the Instruction Cars. The company owned and operated at least three cars during the Streamlined Era. No. 5005, illustrated here, and the 27 were Air Brake Instruction Cars. The 5012 was a Rules Exam Car. (Santa Fe Railway Photo, Kansas State Historical Society Collection)

76

The Business Car "Santa Fe" was the lead car of the fleet. The Santa Fe's portrait was taken at the Los Angeles Union Station and was part of the three car set of Business Cars shown here. The car to the right of the "Santa Fe" appears to be No. 29 but the third car's number is way out of sight. A switch engine has coupled up to the three cars as the group will be part of the consist of an eastbound train later in the day. Business Cars were operated on both regular passenger trains as well as special movements, which were designated as "Passenger Extras." (Santa Fe Railway Photo, John Sward)

The celebration of the *Super C* began in Chicago as well as Los Angeles. The first train included three Business and passenger cars plus a Test Car. Led by No. 100 in the passenger colors, the two FP45s with steam ejecting are blasting thru the banner for an incredible celebrating moment. It was the start of a new era, and it demonstrated the Santa Fe's positive approach for both freight and passenger services to fulfill the needs of shippers and passengers. Although this is a freight train, passenger equipment is part of the picture. What more could one ask for? (Santa Fe Railway Photo, Kansas State Historical Collection)

The *Topeka* was part of the 85 foot streamlined fleet of Business Cars. The cars were superb in every sense of the word. The only thing lacking was the railroad name "Santa Fe" in the letter board. (Santa Fe Railway Photo)

This diagram illustrates the window placement and interior room arrangement of the *Topeka* and *Santa Fe*. (Budd)

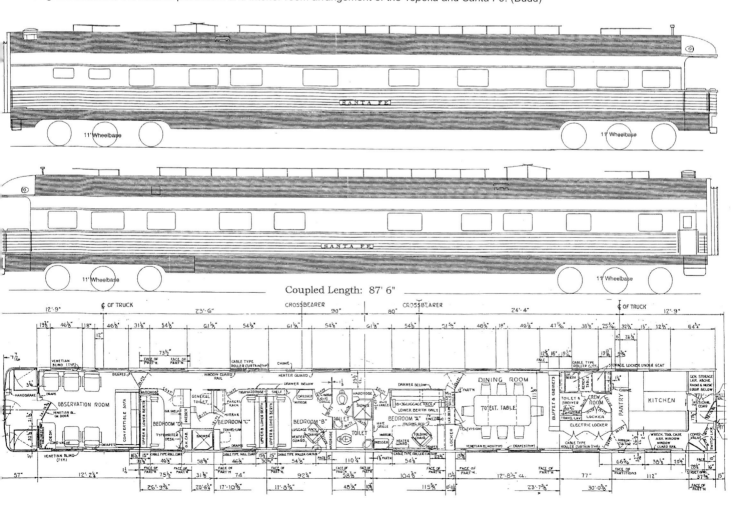

78

Chapter 9 - PASSENGER EQUIPMENT

This chapter is a pictorial review of the Santa Fe passenger equipment operated from the 1940s until Amtrak Day. The company maintained an excellent fleet of standard heavy weight cars, painted in the Pullman Green scheme, as well as a superb fleet of streamlined passengers with an exquisite silver scheme. It can be said that the Santa Fe streamlined equipment stood out with an attractiveness that cannot be described in words. The color scheme of silver and black lettering was a work of art beyond conception.

The following photographs and rosters illustrate the fleet between the 1940s through Amtrak.

The Santa Fe operated a fleet of combination Horse-Express Cars numb from 370 to 376 as well as 377 to 381. When this photo was taken by (Leander in June, 1970, the car was painted in the Santa Fe gray scheme. group was 79 feet, 2 inches long and contained two sections: one for the es and the other for express shipments. Hence one of the reasons for the doors on each side of the car. (J. Michael Gruber Collection)

This is an early Builder's Photo of the Baggage Express Car No. 1829 from the 1585 to 1919 series. The lettering includes the original wording "American Railway Express" which was later changed to "Railway Express Agency." (Santa Fe Railway, Kansas State Historical Society Collection)

SUMMARY OF SANTA FE HEAVYWEIGHT EQUIPMENT DURING THE STREAMLINED ERA THROUGHOUT THE 1940s and 50s.

HEAD-END EQUIPMENT

Type	Number Series	Remark/Seating Cap'y
RPO	57 to 79	60 Foot RPO Section
RPO-Baggage	2000 to 2060	30 Foot RPO Section
RPO-Baggage	2074 to 2087	15 Foot RPO Section
	2100 to 2125	
Box Express Cars	2125 to 2149	
	4100 to 4399	50 Foot cars
	9700 to 9749	
Horse-Express	366 to 370	
	1980 to 1999	
Express-Refrigerator	4000 to 4099	
Baggage Cars Service		Baggage, Mail and Express
	233 to 243	
	1660, 1661	
	1700 to 1853	
	1854 to 1884	
	1890 to 1899	
	1910, 1911	
	1960 to 1979	
	2024 to 2048	

COMBINATION CARS

RPO-Baggage-Coach	111, 112	15 Foot RPO, 65 Seats
Baggage-Coach	2535	36
	2538	32
	2540	20
	2541	32
	2542	64
	2543	37
	2544, 2545	42
	2546	46
	2548	32
	2562	40
	2601	40
	2602 to 2608	26
	2621 to 2623	28
	2644 to 2647	34
	2650	20
	2671	36
	2681, 2682	44
	2694	24
	2698, 2699	28

COACH EQUIPMENT

Coach	483	64
	648	66
	677, 761	72
	780	80

Baggage Car No. 3800 (3800 to 3939) was a smooth side streamlined car with the dark gray paint scheme, 73' 11" long over buffers. The photo was taken after completion at the Topeka Shops. The shells were purchased from the Pullman Company. (Santa Fe Railway Photo, Kansas State Historical Society Collection)

Chair	799 to 804	74		3020 to 3029	57	
Coach	805 to 808	74		3030 to 3069	53	
	809 to 816	76	Chair	3120 to 3132	76	
	824 to 866	76		3133 to 3136	72	
	917 to 999	80	Coach	3303 to 3361	80	
Chair	1000	64		3365 to 3368	80	
	1001	60				
	1002	68	**PARLOR CARS**			
	1010, 1012	72				
	1013	64	Parlor	3209 to 3211	45	
	1014	68		3212, 3213	34	
	1015	64		3217	34	
	1016, 1017	76		3221 to 3223	30	
	1018	72		3224 to 3226	35	
	1020, 1021	66	Parlor - Lounge	3230 to 3233	43	
Chair	1030 to 1037	72				
Chair	1093 to 1099	72	**DINING AND LOUNGE CARS**			
Section						
Chair	1101 to 1127	Rebuilt from 1222	Lounge Dormitory	1350 to 1355	39	
		and 3303; Series	Lounge	1358, 1359	52	
		coaches, 64 seats		1360 to 1369	49	
	1126 to 1141	From 10 Sec., 2	Dining Cars	1400 to 1418	36 or 48	
		Drawing Rm		1435 to 1439	36	
		Sleepers,41 seats		1442 to 1455	30	
				1449	40	
	1155 to 1170	50		1452	36	
	1171 to 1177	Rebuilt from 14		1456 to 1473	36 or 48	
		Sec. Slprs,	Cafe Observation	1508 to 1512	42	
		72 seats		1513, 1514	33	
	1178 to 1197	72	Cafe Lounge	1515, 1516	36	
Chair	1200 to 1221	76	Buffet-Chair Car	1521	59	
Chair	1222 to 1298	72	Lounge-Dormitory	1524 to 1531		
	2964 to 2969	84		1532 to 1537	52	
	2970 to 2999	84				
	3000 to 3019	72				

Fluted side baggage car 3523 (3500 to 3539) was also 73' 10" inches long over buffers. The cars carried the lettering for the Railway Express Agency, and operated continuously on a wide variety of passenger trains, although most often in streamlined consists. (Santa Fe Railway Photo, Kansas State Historical Society Collection)

Baggage car 3451 (3432 to 3452, 73' 8" long over buffers) carried lettering for both the Railway Express Agency as well as the word "Baggage" in the center of the car. The 3451's portrait was taken at the Los Angeles Union Station and was being set for loading prior to its run to Chicago. (Santa Fe Railway Photo, Kansas State Historical Society Collection)

SLEEPING CARS

Heavyweight Pullman Cars

The Santa Fe operated a variety of Pullman cars throughout its history. However, most if not all of the cars were owned by the Pullman Company.

14 Sections

Cyrus Field
George Stephenson
Isaae Newton
James Watt

John Stevens
Louis Pasteur
Samuel Bard

8 Sections, 2 Compartments, 1 Drawing Room - Cent. . . Series

Centacre	Centello	Centoak	Centsylvia
Centamia	Centgate	Centosa	Centwell
Centanda	Centholm	Centpaulo	Laurel Valley
Centarch	Centlawn	Centguora	Laurel Wood
Centash	Centlea	Centrail	
Centaya	Centioch	Centrange	
Centcampo	Centlow	Centrock	
Centdale	Centnome	Centshire	

10 Sections Lounge - General Series

General Carr
General Chaffee
General Crook
General Hancock
General Howard

General Kearney
General Lawton
General Mills
General Schofield
General Stoneman

3 Drawing Rooms, 6 Compartments - Glen Series

Glen Beach	Glen Forge	Glen Terrace
Glen Delta	Glen Frazer	Oconomowoc
Glen Ewen	Glen Roberts	Okauchee

10 Sections, 1 Drawing Room, 2 Compartments - Lake Series

Dean Lake	Lava Lake	Star Lake
Dell Lake	Lone Lake	Swan Lake
Echo Lake	Moose Lake	
Fern Lake	Spear Lake	

6 Sections, 1 Drawing Room, 4 Double Bedrooms - Tribe Series

Attakapa Tribe	Hopi Tribe	Shoshone Tribe
Choctaw Tribe	Kaw Tribe	
Comanche Tribe	Kiowa Tribe	

MIXED TRAIN EQUIPMENT

Coach Baggage	3200 to 2308	36
Caboose Cars	2310 to 2314	14
	2315, 2316	28
	2318	44
	2320	32
	2322	30
	2324, 2325	28
	2330 to 2381	36
	2383	34
	2384	28

Sixty foot Rail Post Office Car No. 59 was part of the 57 to 79 series. The 59 was built in 1928 and saw operation well into the Streamlined Era. (Santa Fe Railway Photo, Kansas State Historical Society Collection)

This portrait of the No. 60 illustrates the opposite side as shown with car No. 59. No. 60 was photographed at Marceline, Missouri in May, 1968. (Harold K. Vollrath Collection)

MIXED TRAIN EQUIP. (CONTINUED)

	2386	36
	2395	34
	2396	36
	2397	32
	2401	30
	2402 to 2412	28 and 36
	2415	32
	2420	30
	2421 to 2425	28 to 36
	2535	36
	2538	32
	2540	20
	2541	32
	2542	64
	2543	37
	2544 to 2546	42 and 46
	2548	32

STEAM GENERATOR CARS

Number Series	Remarks
1 to 5	Rebuilt from Locomotive Tenders

Note: Many of the heavy weight cars continued operation throughout the 1960s and were often used for extra service for a variety of passenger operations. Heavy weight head-end cars continued in operation until most of the mail contracts were pulled away from the U.S. railroads. The heavy weight equipment is just one example of durability of railroad equipment and long lasting effectiveness over decades as well as meeting service needs.

RPO No. 75 (70 to 79) was built by the Pullman Company in 1927. (Santa Fe Railway, Kansas State Historical Society Collection)

Streamlined smooth side Railway Post Office Car No. 51 (50 to 52) was 63' 10" long over buffers. The cars had very small lettering in the center of the car, "United States Mail Railway Post Office." (Owen Leander, J. Michael Gruber Collection)

STREAMLINED EQUIPMENT ROSTER

HEAD-END EQUIPMENT

Type	No. Series Or Names	Length Over Buffers	Seating Cap'y	Remarks
RPO	50 to 52	63' 10"		60' RPO
	57 to 79	64' 3"		60' RPO
	80, 81	63' 2"		60' RPO
	82 to 88	63' 10"		60' RPO
	89 to 98	64'		60' RPO
	99 to 110	63' 3"		60' RPO
RPO-Baggage	3400 to 3408	73' 10"		30' RPO
Baggage	3409 to 3426	73' 10"		
	3430	80' 4"		
	3431	63' 8"		
	3432 to 3452	73' 8"		
	3438	73' 10"		
	3432 to 3452	73' 8"		
	3453 to 3466	73' 10"		
	3500 to 3539	73' 10"		
	3540 to 3554	73' 10"		
RPO-Baggage	3600 to 3606	73' 10"		30' RPO
Baggage	3650 to 3660	73' 10"		
	3662 to 3684	73' 10"		
	3700 to 3799	63' 11"		
	3800 to 3939	73' 11"		
	3990 to 3999	73' 11"		
Container Flats	200 to 230			Large End Doors Handling Container Shipments of Mail

COMBINATION CARS

Baggage-Chair	3490, 3491	80' 4"	36
	3492, 3493	80' 4"	38

RPO Car No. 87 (82 to 88) was 64' 3" long over buffers. Photographed at Marceline, Missouri in May, 1968. (Harold K. Vollrath Collection)

BAGGAGE DORMITORY CARS

Baggage-Dorm	1380 to 1387	79' 10"		
Baggage-Dorm	3472	79' 10"		
	3473	81' 6"		
	3476	79' 10"		
	3477 to 3479	85'		
	3480, 3481	80' 4"		
Baggage-Dorm-Chair	3482	80' 4"	28	Rebuilt to Baggage Dorm

Note: Cars 3477 to 3482 converted with Hi-level Adapter for Hi-Level El Capitan Service

COACH EQUIPMENT

Hi-levlel Chair Cars	526, 527	85'	68	
	528 to 549	85'	68	
	700 to 736	85'	72	
Chair Cars	1100	85'	56	Pendulum
	2791 to 2793	85'	48	

2794 to 2815	84' 6"	48	
2816 to 2860	85'	48	
2861 to 2945	85'	44	
2946, 2947	80'	44	
2948, 2949	79' 10"	44	
2950 to 2955	84' 6"	44	
2956	79' 10	44	
2957 to 2959	79' 10"	44	
2960	80'	44	
3070	79' 6"	63	Converted to 52 Seats
3071	79' 8"	63	"

Club Lounge	1388, 1389	79' 8"	47
Lounge-Dorm	1390 to 1395	79' 8"	27
Diner-Lounge	1396, 1397	79' 9"	47
Club-Chair	1398, 1399	79' 10"	56
Dining Cars	1474 to 1485	83' 2"	36
	1486, 1487	83' 2"	48

RPO No. 102 was part of the 99 to 110 series. (Owen Leander, J. Michael Gruber Collection)

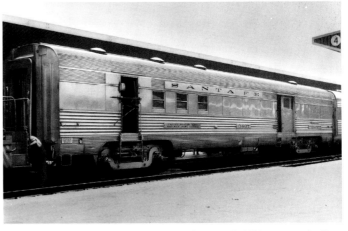

RPO-Baggage No. 3407 (3400 to 3408) was 73' 10" long over buffers. The group served on trains that required a 30 foot Railway Post Office section for the mail traffic. (Santa Fe Railway, Kansas State Historical Society Collection)

	3072 to 3101	79' 10"	60	"
	3102	79' 10"	48	
	3103 to 3116	79' 10"	52	
	3119		52	
	3137 to 3166	83' 10"	60	Converted to 42 Seats
	3187 to 3189	85'	50	
Chair-	3197	85'	38	
Observation	3198, 3199		38	
	3240		60	
	3243, 3244		60	
	3245		60	
	3246 to 3248		42	
Parlor-	3241, 3242		32	
Observation				

	1488	83' 2"	36	
	1489 to 1498	83'	36	
Lunch Counter	1500 to 1502	83' 2 "	37	
1501 converted to Cafeteria Car				
Diner	1503, 1504	83'	38	
	1505, 1506	83' 2"	38	
	1507	83' 2"	38	
	1550 to 1565	85'	40	
	1566 to 1568	85'	32	
	1569 to 1577	85'	21	
Includes Dormitory Section				
Club-Chair	3117, 3118	79' 10"	59	
Chair-				
Lounge Car	3179	85'	56	

DINING AND LOUNGE CARS

Dome Lounge	500 to 505	86' 6"	57	
Dome Lounge	506 to 513	85'	103	Equipped with Coach Seats
Chair	526, 527			
	550 to 555			
Lounge	575 to 580	85'		Hi-level Lounge Car
Dining Cars	600 to 606	85'	36	
	650 to 655	85'	80	Hi-level Dining Cars
Club Lounge	1339 to 1344	85'	28	
Dormitory	1345	85'	32	
Club Lounge	1346	85'	48	
	1347 to 1349	85'	50	
Club Lounge	1370 to 1378	79' 10"	27 or 29	
Club Baggage	1380 to 1385	79' 10"	29	
Baggage-Lounge	1386, 1387	79' 10"	32	

PULLMAN SLEEPING CARS

10 Roomette, 6 Double Bedroom Cars - Pine Series

Pine Arroyo	Pine Dale	Pine Leaf
Pine Beach	Pine Dawn	Pine Lodge
Pine Bell	Pine Fern	Pine Mesa
Pine Bluff	Pine Gem	Pine Pass
Pine Brook	Pine Gorge	Pine Peak
Pine Cavern	Pine Grove	Pine Range
Pine Cove	Pine Hill	Pine Rapids
Pine Creek	Pine Island	Pine Ring
Pine Crest	Pine King	Pine Shore

10 Roomette, 6 Double Bedroom Cars - Palm Series

Palm Arch	Palm Lore	Palm Top
Palm Dome	Palm Path	Palm Tower
Palm Haven	Palm Star	Palm View
Palm Leaf	Palm Stream	
Palm Loch	Palm Summit	

24 Duplex Roomette Cars - Indian Series - Built 1947

Indian Arrow	Indian Flute	Indian Pony
Indian Canoe	Indian Lake	Indian Scout
Indian Drum	Indian Maid	Indian Song

Indian Falls   Indian Mesa   Indian Squaw

11 Double Bedroom Cars - Indian Series

The 11 Double Bedroom Cars were rebuilt from the 24 Duplex Roomette Sleepers in 1964 and continued to carry the original names as listed above.

4 Compartments, 4 Double Bedrooms, 2 Drawing Rooms - Regal Series

Regal Arms	Regal Crown	Regal Hunt	Regal Ring
Regal Center	Regal Dome	Regal Inn	Regal River
Regal City	Regal Elm	Regal Isle	Regal Ruby
Regal Corps	Regal Gate	Regal Lane	Regal Spa
Regal Court	Regal Gorge	Regal Lark	Regal Stream
Regal Creek	Regal Gulf	Regal Manor	Regal Temple
Regal Crest	Regal Hill	Regal Oak	Regal Town
Regal Cross	Regal House	Regal Pass	Regal Vale

4 Compartments, 4 Double Bedrooms, 2 Drawing Rooms

Bacobi	Kaibito	Mohave	Saydotah
Hasta	Kayenta	Nankoweap	Seboyeta
Hotevilla	Kietsiel	Naslini	Tchirege
Hualpai	Klethla	Nava	Tsankawi
Jadito	Moencopi	Polacca	

10 Roomettes, 3 Double Bedrooms, 2 Compartments - Blue Series

Blue Bay	Blue Grove	Blue Lake	Blue Pond
Blue Bell	Blue Heart	Blue Moon	Blue Ridge
Blue Flag	Blue Heron	Blue Mott	Blue Spring
Blue Gem	Blue Hill	Blue Mound	Blue Water
Blue Grass	Blue Island	Blue Point	

4 Drawing Rooms, 1 Double Bedroom, Observation Car - Vista Series

Vista Canyon	Vista Cavern	Vista Heights
Vista Valley	Vista Club	Vista Plains

4 Drawing Rooms, 1 Double Bedroom, Observation Car

Betahtakin	Chuska
Biltabito	Donehotso
Chaistla	Puye

8 Section, 1 Drawing Room, 2 Compartment Car

Isleta   Laguna

2 Drawing Rooms, 1 Double Bedroom, 3 Compartments,

Observation Car -

Navajo

6 Double Bedrooms, 2 Compartments, 2 Drawing Rooms

Oraibi   Taos

8 Sections, 2 Compartments and 2 Double Bedrooms

Forward

6 Sections, 6 Roomettes, 4 Double Bedrooms - Valley Series

Antelope Valley	Monument Valley	San Migual Valley
Blue Valley	Paradise Valley	Sunshine Valley
Chama Valley	Pecos Valley	Surprise Valley
Cimmaron Valley	Pleasant Valley	Sweetwater Valley
Cottonwood Valley	Redondo Valley	Taos Valley
Eagle Nest Valley	Red River Valley	Tesuque Valley
Hidden Valley	Red Rock Valley	Verge Valley
Kaw Valley	Rio Grande Valley	Whitewater Valley
Mescalero Valley	Salt River Valley	

17 Roomettes, 1 Section Car

Chaeo	Otowi
Chimayo	Paria
Chinie	Tonto
Matto	Tuba

10 Roomettes, 5 Double Bedrooms - Cascade Series

Cascade Mills   Cascade Shoals

14 Section Car

Dinnebito	Havasu
Ganado	Hoskinnini
Hakatai	Hotauta

8 Sections, 2 Compartments and 2 Double Bedrooms

Salahkai	Toadiena	Tonalea	Tyuonyi
Segatoa	Tohatchi	Toreva	Wupatki
Shanto	Tolani	Toroweap	Yampai
Talwiwi	Tolchico	Tyende	

Steam Generator Cars

Number Series	Remarks
131 to 140	Rebuilt from 3915 series baggage cars

Standard Heavyweight Combine No. 2603 (2602 to 2608) is shown here with its number painted out at Marceline, Missouri in May, 1968. This group of cars was used as the prototype for the combination cars produced in HO gauge by IHC. (Harold K. Vollrath Collection)

Still another example of the rebuilt cars was the 3041 (3030 to 3069). Again the number has been painted out as the car is in the retirement line at Marceline. (Harold K. Vollrath Collection)

A Coach that was similar to the previous car illustrated was the Coach Club car No. 1535 (1532 to 1537). However, the window configuration is a bit different. Note the smaller window to the left of the words "Coach Club". (Santa Fe Railway, Kansas State Historical Society Collection)

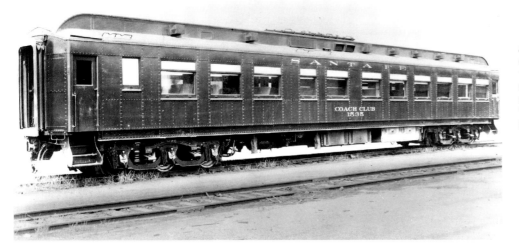

Chair Car 2930 was part of the series 2861 to 2945. This group of Chair Cars were built for the *El Capitan* with 44 leg rest seating. (Santa Fe Railway, Kansas State Historical Society Collection)

A rather interesting combination car was the No. 92 (and the 91) which were RPO-Smoker cars. The cars contained a 15 foot Railway Post Office section and provided seating for 65 passengers. The 92 was photographed at Los Angeles between runs. (Santa Fe Railway, Kansas State Historical Society Collection)

The Santa Fe operated a wide fleet of Dormitory Baggage cars for the transcontinental streamliners. The 3482 was originally a combination Baggage Dormitory Chair Car. The car was later rebuilt with an extended profile roof at one end to match the Hi-level Chair Cars built for the *El Capitan*. (Owen Leander, J. Michael Gruber Collection)

Standard Heavyweight Coach No. 3017 (3000 to 3019) was rebuilt with picture windows. The car was photographed in the retirement line at Marceline, Missouri in May, 1968. (Harold K. Vollrath Collection)

Chair Car 3071 was a smooth side 63 seat coach, 79' 8" long over the buffers. (J. Michael Gruber Collection)

Chair Car 3163 provided seating for 60 passengers and was 83' 10" long over the buffers. (Santa Fe Railway, Kansas State Historical Society Collection)

Heavyweight car No. 1348 was designated a Buffet Library Car named the *San Vincente*. The car was a combination car with a baggage section, and the service provided includes snacks and a library section for a variety of books for reading relaxation while traveling "All the Way on the Santa Fe." (Santa Fe Railway, Kansas State Historical Society Collection)

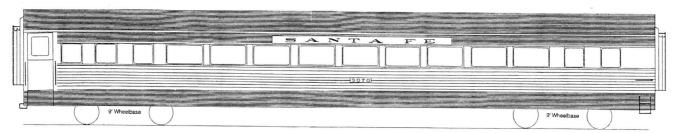

Coupled Length: 79' 2", Buffer Bolster: 13' 1"

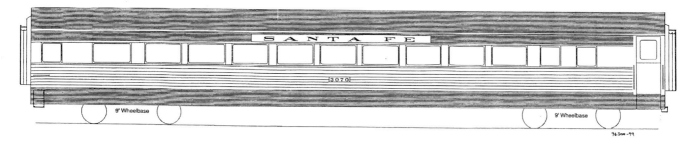

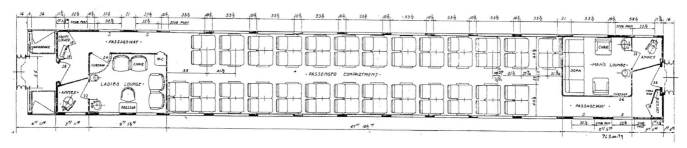

This diagram illustrates the streamlined coach 3070, which was built by Budd in January, 1936, as a test car for the new light weight concepts. (Budd)

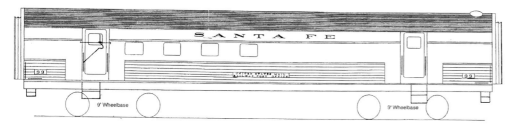

Coupled Length: 63' 3"

Budd built RPO Cars, 99 to 110, delivered in 1964. (Budd)

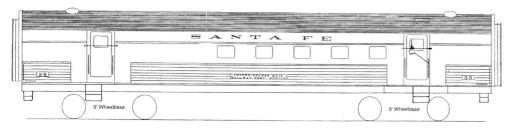

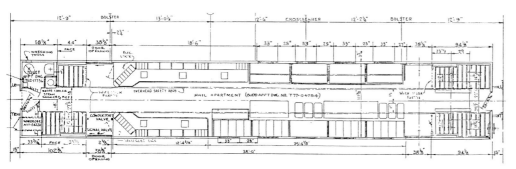

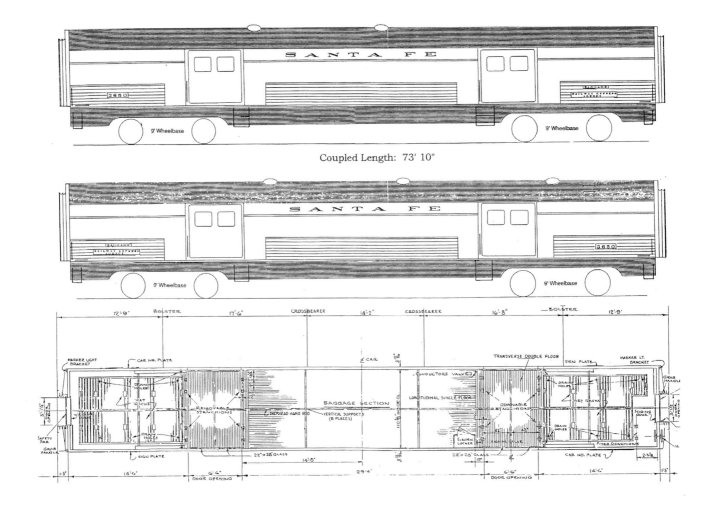

Coupled Length: 73' 10"

Diagram illustrating the 73' 10 Baggage Cars, 3500 to 3539 and 3540 to 3554, built by Budd in 1953 and 1957 respectively. (Budd)

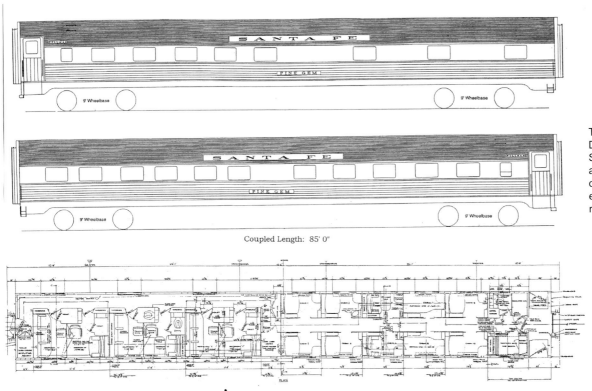

Coupled Length: 85' 0"

The 10 Roomette, 6 Double Bedroom Sleeping Cars were among the most common of the streamlined sleepers throughout the railroad industry. (Budd)

Chair Car 2871 (2861 to 2945) was a 44 seat leg-rest coach. The car was built in 1947. (Santa Fe Railway Photo, Kansas State Historical Society Collection)

Hi-level Chair Cars were originally operated on the *El Capitan*, but also served on the San Francisco Chief when additional equipment was purchased. Chair Car 700 was part of the 700 to 736 series built by the Budd Company. The cars were equipped with leg rest seating for 72 passengers. (Santa Fe Railway, Kansas State Historical Society Collection)

One of the more unusual Chair Cars to be acquired by the Santa Fe was the Hill Pendulum type car. The Great Northern, Burlington and Santa Fe experimented with this type of equipment. However, none of the three railroads went beyond the experimental stage with the idea. Note the type of windows on the No. 1100. (Santa Fe Railway, Patrick C. Dorin Collection)

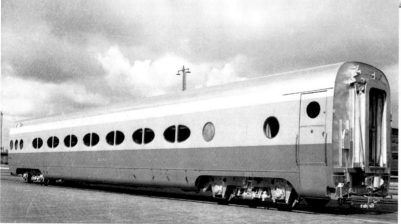

Cafe Lounge Car No. 1515 (and 1516) were built by Pullman in May, 1931. The cars provided seating for 36 passengers for meal, snacks, and beverage service. (Santa Fe Railway, Kansas State Historical Society Collection)

Dining Car 1406 (1402 to 1411) was built by the Pullman Company in December, 1927. The cars provided seating for 36 or 48 passengers depending upon the seating arrangement within the individual cars. (Santa Fe Railway, Kansas State Historical Society Collection)

This photo shows the 1407 after rebuilding and modifying the window structure as compared to the 1406 in the previous photo. This view shows the opposite of the 1402 to 1411 series. (Rail Photo Service, Patrick C. Dorin Collection)

The Santa Fe rebuilt many of the heavyweight cars and painted them to match the streamlined fluted side equipment. Just one example is the Lounge Car No. 1361, the San Dieguito, which provided snack and beverage service with seating for 49 passengers. (Santa Fe Railway, Harry Stegmaier Collection)

Moving into the Streamlined Equipment, we have Dining Car No. 603 from the 600 to 606 series. This group of dining cars was originally assigned to the Super Chief and provided seating for 36 passengers. (Owen Leander, J. Michael Gruber Collection)

Dining Car 1485 (1474 to 1485) was named the Awatobi and provided seating for 36 passengers. (Santa Fe Railway, Kansas State Historical Society Collection)

Car No. 1556 (1550 to 1565) was a superb Lunch Counter Diner with seating for 40 passengers. The equipment was assigned to the *Chief* and the *San Francisco Chief*. (Santa Fe Railway, Kansas State Historical Society Collection)

Car No. 1567 (1566 to 1568) was still another version of the Lunch Counter Diners operated by the Santa Fe. (Harold K. Vollrath Collection)

Hi-level Dining Cars were part of the consist the new *El Capitan*. No. 651 was part of the 650 to 655 series. (Santa Fe Railway, Kansas State Historical Society Collection)

Car No. 1380 (1380 to 1385) was a Club Baggage car with seating for 29 passengers. This group was 79' 10" long over the buffers. The car was named the San Miguel. Technically, the cars were named Baggage-Barber Shop-Buffet Lounge Cars, built by the Budd Company in 1937 and originally assigned to the *Super Chief*. (Owen Leander, J. Michael Gruber Collection)

Lounge Car 1391 was a 79' 8" long car over the buffers and included a dormitory section for crews. (Owen Leander, J. Michael Gruber)

Pleasure Dome Lounge Car No. 501 was built for the *Super Chief* (Series 500 to 505). The cars were built by the Pullman Company in 1950 and operated exclusively on the *Super Chief*. (Santa Fe Railway, Patrick C. Dorin Collection)

Big Dome Lounge Car No. 507 (506 to 513) provided service on the Chief as well as the *San Francisco Chief* and the *Chicagoan* and the *Kansas Cityan* between Chicago and Oklahoma City. (Santa Fe Railway, Patrick C. Dorin Collection)

Big Dome 550 (550 to 555)

The Nava was a 4 Compartment, 2 Drawing Room and 4 Double Bedroom sleeping car built by Pullman in 1939. Eventually in the early 1960s, the car was transferred to "Dormitory Car" service and renumbered 3487. Note that the car carried only the Pullman name in the letter board. (Santa Fe Railway, Kansas State Historical Society Collection)

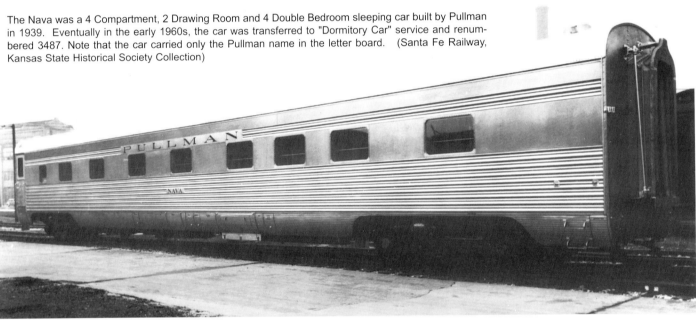

The *Paria* was part of the same group as the Tuba built by Pullman in 1938. In this photo, the car is lettered only for Pullman. The group carried Indian exotic names. (Santa Fe Railway, Kansas State Historical Society Collection)

The Pullman Car *Yampai* was an 8 section, 2 Compartments and 2 Double Bedroom car which included windows for the upper berths. (Santa Fe Railway, Kansas State Historical Society Collection)

The *Tuba* was a 17 Roomette, 1 Section sleeping car, which was part of the fleet assigned to Super Chief during part of its career. The car was lettered for the Santa Fe with the sub-lettering Pullman next to the vestibule. (Santa Fe Railway, Harry Stegmaier Collection)

Not all Santa Fe passenger cars carried fluted sides. A number of Pullman cars as well as other equipment were smooth side cars. One example with the sleeping car fleet were the Valley series 6 Section, 6 Roomette, 4 Double Bedroom cars, such as the *Sunshine Valley* shown here at Chicago. The car was painted a dark gray with white lettering which included "Santa Fe" in the letter board with Pullman sub-lettering next to the vestibule. (Owen Leander, J. Michael Gruber Collection)

The Indian Series were originally built as 24 Duplex Roomette Sleeping Cars. (Santa Fe Railway, Harry Stegmaier Collection)

In 1964, the Santa Fe rebuilt the Indian Series cars to 11 Double Bedroom cars and did not change the car names. (Santa Fe Railway, Harry Stegmaier)

The *Pine Beach* was part of the Pine Series 10 Roomette, 6 Double Bedroom Sleeping Car fleet built by the Budd Company in 1949-50. (Santa Fe Railway, Kansas State Historical Society Collection)

The Palm series, such as the Palm Arch were also 10 Roomette, 6 Double Bedroom cars which were built by American Car and Foundry. (Santa Fe Railway, Kansas State Historical Society Collection)

The Blue Series were built by the Pullman Company with 10 Roomettes, 2 Compartments, and 3 Double Bedrooms. (Santa Fe Railway, Kansas State Historical Society Collection)

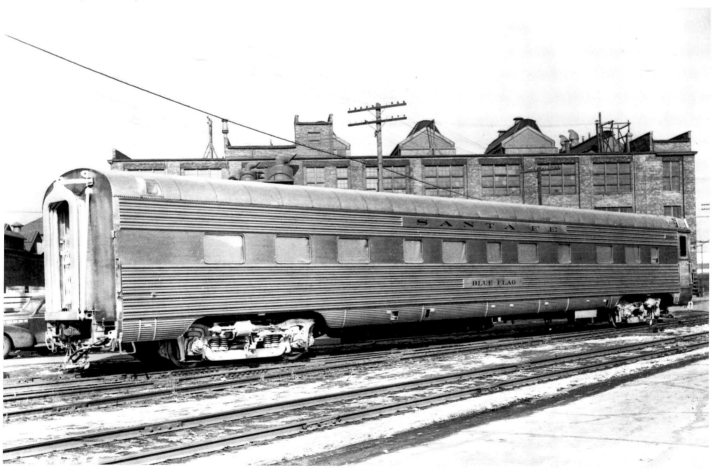

Still another example of exotic Indian names was the *Polacca*, which was built by Pullman in 1938. The accommodations included 4 Compartments, 2 Drawing Rooms and 4 Double Bedrooms. (Santa Fe Railway, Harry Stegmaier Collection)

The Pullman Company built the Regal Series 4 Compartment, 2 Drawing Rooms and 4 Double Bedroom cars in 1948, such as the Regal Court illustrated here. (Santa Fe Railway, Kansas State Historical Society Collection)

The Santa Fe owned and operated three Parlor Observation Cars built by the Pullman Company in 1927. The cars were numbered 3224 to 3226. (Santa Fe Railway, Kansas State Historical Society)

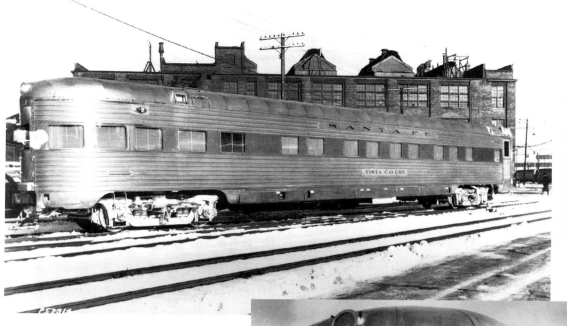

The Observation Sleeping Car *Vista Cavern* was one of a group of 6 cars sent to Pullman in 1956 to have the rounded ends squared off for mid-train operation. This photo shows the *Vista Cavern* with a batch of snow on the rear end of the car. (Santa Fe Railway, Kansas State Historical Society Collection)

The Budd Company built 5 Observation Parlor Cars in 1938, number series 3240 to 3245. Two were assigned to the *Kansas Cityan* and the *Chicagoan*, and later to the *Tulsan*. The 3240, 3243 and the 3244 were converted to Observation Chair Cars almost immediately after delivery in 1938, and were assigned to the *Golden Gates* at the same time. (Santa Fe Railway, Kansas State Historical Society Collection)

The Pullman car *Chastla*, which operated on the *San Francisco Chief,* had been converted from a round end observation car to a squared end car complete with end windows as can be observed from the top down photo. The car was designated a Lounge - Sleeping Car. Note the Santa Fe box cars in the background with "Ship and Travel Santa Fe All the Way." (Santa Fe Railway, Harry Stegmaier Collection)

100

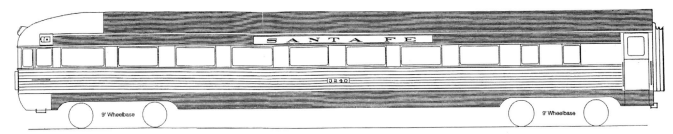

Coupled Length: 80' 0", Buffer Bolster: 12' 11", Rear 12' 7"

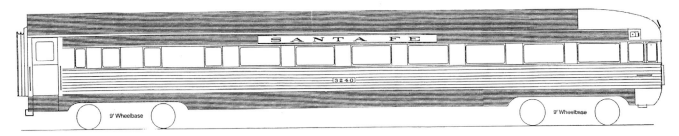

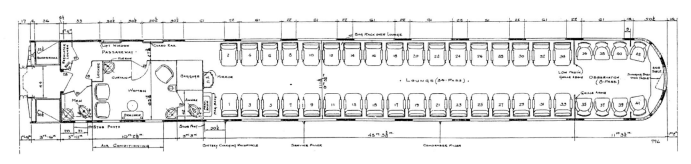

Diagram illustrating the Budd Build Observation Parlor Cars, 3240 to 3245. (Budd)

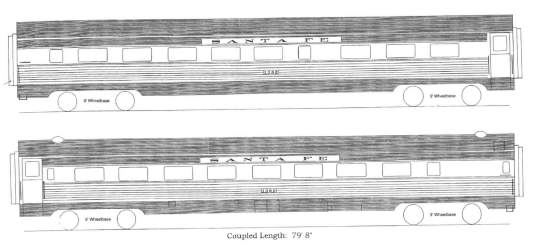

Coupled Length: 79' 8"

Still another innovation was the Coach Bar Lounge Cars, such as 1396 and 1397, built by Budd in 1940. The cars were originally built for the *El Capitan*. Eventually they were reconfigured to full lounge cars in 1940, and converted to Diner Lounge cars for the *Kansas City Chief* in 1952. (Budd)

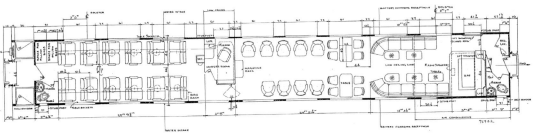

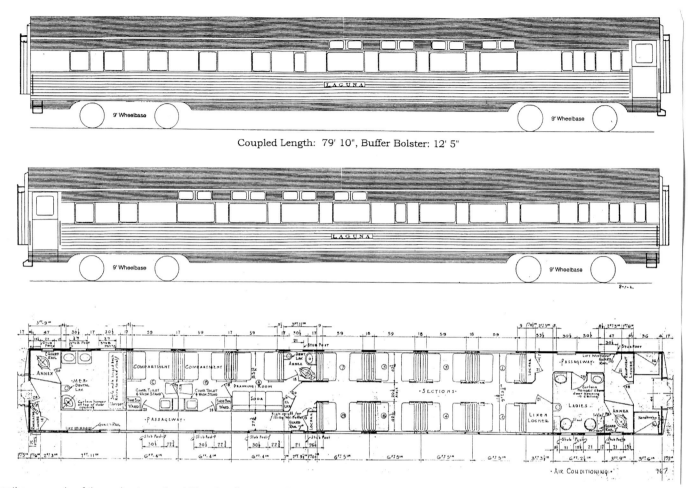

Coupled Length: 79' 10", Buffer Bolster: 12' 5"

Another example of the early streamlined Sleeping Cars were the 8 section, 2 compartment and 1 drawing room cars built by Budd in 1937. They were patterned after the standard heavy weight 8-2-1 cars and one can say the concept continued to roll. (Budd)

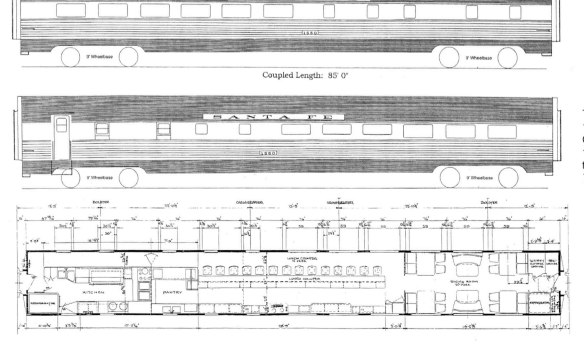

Coupled Length: 85' 0"

The Budd Company built 16 Lunch Counter Dining Car, number series 1550 to 1565, in 1948 for service on the *El Capitan* and the *Texas Chief*. (Budd)

Chapter 10 - PASSENGER MOTIVE POWER

It goes without saying that the Santa Fe owned and operated a very powerful, artistically designed, colorful and fast passenger motive power through the Steam Days to Amtrak. Ranging from small and light 4-4-2s to the big 4-8-4s, the Santa Fe steam could do the job of handling passengers between Chicago and the West Coast, and all points in between.

Diesel power began its career on the Santa Fe in the 1930s with the introduction of the *Super Chief* and the development of a fleet of *Chiefs* throughout the territory. The color scheme of the Santa Fe passenger power will never be forgotten. In fact, it continued to exist through the Burlington Northern Santa Fe merger.

This chapter is a pictorial review of the steam and diesel passenger power owned and operated by the railroad. The Santa Fe's positive image could not be mistaken when viewing a 4 unit system on the head-end of a *Super Chief*, the *El Capitan* or any of the other *Chiefs* and other passenger operations. What made the this image so impressive was that it matched the positive atmosphere of the railroad for passengers and shippers.

A SUMMARY OF PASSENGER MOTIVE POWER

The following steam and diesel locomotive rosters are an overview of the types of motive power in passenger service during the "Streamlined Era" from the mid-1930s thru to the Amtrak Era.

STEAM POWER

Type	Class	Number Series
4-4-2	256	256 to 259
	454	454 to 463
	507	507 to 541
	542	542 to 559
	1400	1400 to 1451
	1452	1452 to 1479
	1480	1480 to 1502
	1550	1550 to 1561
4-6-2	1200	1200 to 1225 (1207, 1210, 1214 and 1215 were 2-6-2s)
	1226	1226 to 1266
	1270	1270 to 1289
	1290	1290 to 1296
	1297	1297 to 1308
	1309	1309 to 1336
	1398	1398, 1399
	3400	3400 to 3449
	3500	3500 to 3534
	3600	3600
4-6-4	3450	3450 to 3459
	3460	3460 to 3465
4-8-2	3700	3700 to 3750
4-8-4	2900	2900 to 2929
	3751	3751 to 3764
	3765	3765 to 3775
	3776	3776 to 3785

For a detailed history of Santa Fe steam power including builders, dates built and scrapped, the reader may wish to refer to the book IRON HORSES OF THE SANTA FE TRAIL By E. D. Worley.

The Santa Fe streamlined the 4-6-4 Hudson, No. 3460, powered the *Chief* and other high speed trains between Chicago and La Junta, Colorado. With a balanced artistic appearance, the 3460 sent out the word that travel on the Santa Fe was the way to go. (Santa Fe Railway Photo)

DIESEL POWER

Class	Type	Number Series	HP	Bldr	Year	Remarks
1	E1	1	1800	EMC	1935	2 unit set. Rebuilt to E8ms # 83 and 84 in 1953
2	E1	2 to 4	1800	EMC	1937-38	2 unit sets
	E1	5 to 9	1800		1938	1 unit, all rebuilt to E8ms, 80 series in 1953
11	E3	11	2000	EMD	1939	2 unit set
	E6	12, 13	2000		1940-41	2 unit sets
	E6	14	2000		1940	1 unit
	E6	15	2000		1941	2 unit set
100	FT	142 to 168	1350	EMD	1944-45	11 4 unit sets converted from freight
16	F3	16 to 36	1500	EMD	1946-49	4 unit sets
37	F7	37 to 47	1500	EMD	1949-52	4 unit sets No. 32A was rebuilt and Renumbered 48A
80	E8m	80 to 84	2000	EMD	1952-53	2 unit sets
		85 to 87	2000		1953	1 unit Rebuilt from E1s
300	F7	300 to 314	1500	EMD	1952-53	3 unit sets
325	F7	325 to 340	1500	EMD	1950-53	3 unit sets
		341 to 344				2 unit sets
100	FP45	100 to 108	3600	EMD	1967	
350	U28CG	350 to 359	2800	GE	1966	
400	U30CG	400 to 405	3000	GE	1967	Cowl Units
50	PA	50	2000	Alco	1941	2 unit set
51	PA1	51	2000	Alco	1946	3 unit set
52	PA2	52 to 62	2000	Alco	1946-48	2 unit sets
		64 to 69				1 unit set
		70 to 73				2 unit sets

Note: Single units 58 to 62 were renumbered 74 to 78

Class	Type	Number Series	HP	Bldr	Year	Remarks
90	Erie	90	2000	FM	1947	3 unit set

Road-switchers with Steam Generators

Class	Type		Number Series	HP	Bldr	Year	Remarks
600	RSD-7	600, 601	2250	Alco	1955		
2099	RS-3		2099	1600	Alco	1950	
2100	RSD-5		2152 to 2156	1600	Alco	1953	
2650	GP-7		2650 to 2654	1500	EMD	1950	
			2879 to 2893	1500		1953	Contained both a steam generator and dynamic brakes

Switch Engines with Steam Generators

Class	Type	Number Series	HP	Bldr	Year	Remarks
541	H12-44TS	541 to 543	1200	FM	1956	These three units were built on road-switcher under-frames.

The beginning of the diesel era with and for the Santa Fe passenger services began with the 1800 horsepower No. 1. The unit is being prepared for its first trip with the *Chief*. The date is September 13, 1935 - a red number day for launching a new Era on the Santa Fe leading into the Streamlined Era. (William S. Kuba Collection)

The streamlined era is underway and is simultaneous with the vast majority of steam powered passenger trains. No. 1431, a 4-4-2, is heading up a local passenger train on the main line of the Illinois Division. It has just taken on water during its stop at Chillicothe, Illinois in this February, 1943 portrait. The 1431 was built by Baldwin in 1907. (Harold K. Vollrath Collection)

The next step in part of the motive power development history was the 4-6-4 Hudson. This type of locomotive was operated by many railroads for its passenger power effectiveness with a larger boiler / firebox supported by a 4 wheel truck beneath the cab. The 4-6-4 Hudsons handled many of the prime Santa Fe passenger trains during the steam era and well into the Streamlined Era. The 3452 was built by Baldwin in 1927, and is shown here 20 years later in full service at Kansas City in December, 1947. (Harold K. Vollrath Collection)

The primary motive power for passenger-trains for many years was the 4-6-2 Pacifc. One example was the 1218 between runs at San Bernadino, Calif. in Dec. 1935. The 1218 was built by Baldwin in 1903. (Harold K. Vollrath Collection)

The 4-8-2 Mountain type traveled system wide with many Santa Fe trains well into the Streamlined Era. A passenger F unit is in the background of the 3735 between runs at Los Angeles in June, 1950. The days of its career are numbered but it is still providing first class passenger service for the Santa Fe. The 3735 was built by Baldwin in 1921. (Harold K. Vollrath Collection)

Steam power did the job with a sense of romance that could never be found in any other type of industry. Mountain 4-8-2 No. 3746 is leading the 4-8-4 No. 3783 on an Arizona Grade near Nelson, Arizona in September, 1941. (James Bowie Photo, William S. Kuba Collection)

Some of the largest passenger motive power were the 4-8-4s, such as the 3751 in this photo between runs at Los Angeles in May, 1950. This engine was built by Baldwin in 1927 and had an incredible career handling all types of passenger trains well into the Streamlined Era. (Harold K. Vollrath Collection)

The Barstow Diesel Shops served a wide variety of motive power on the far western end of the Santa Fe. This photo illustrates three types of passenger power. In the foreground we have a four unit set of F3s. It is easy to see the steam generator exhaust system on the top of the B units. Note the single headlight in the nose of No. 18. Next is a set of FT freight units, but on the next track is a four unit set of rebuilt FTs with steam generators in the B units and painted in the passenger colors. The 158 is leading the pack. The next set of passenger power is a three unit set of Alco PAs. (Santa Fe Railway Photo)

The No. 1 has been rebuilt and it is leading a west-bound 7 car streamlined train at Galesburg, Illinois. (William S. Kuba Collection)

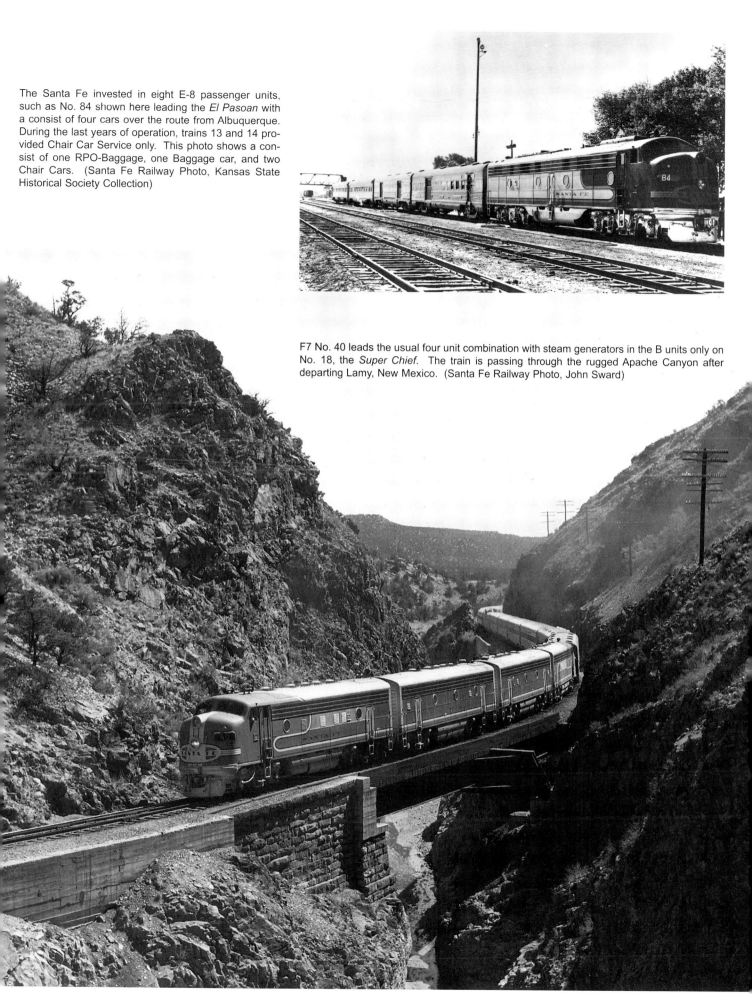

The Santa Fe invested in eight E-8 passenger units, such as No. 84 shown here leading the *El Pasoan* with a consist of four cars over the route from Albuquerque. During the last years of operation, trains 13 and 14 provided Chair Car Service only. This photo shows a consist of one RPO-Baggage, one Baggage car, and two Chair Cars. (Santa Fe Railway Photo, Kansas State Historical Society Collection)

F7 No. 40 leads the usual four unit combination with steam generators in the B units only on No. 18, the *Super Chief*. The train is passing through the rugged Apache Canyon after departing Lamy, New Mexico. (Santa Fe Railway Photo, John Sward)

Below: The Santa Fe purchased one DL-109 from Alco, the No. 50. This side view illustrates the paint application on these units with the artistic long nose. (Bob's Photos)

No. 4 is an E1A built by Electro-Motive in 1938. It is shown here leading the *Chief* at Chillicothie, Illinois. (Collection of John A Rehor)

FT No. 167 was the only set of FTs built new as passenger power. There were a grand total of 11 sets of FTs in passenger service. The 167 is leading a train with both heavy weight and streamlined equipment at Pasadena, California in 1946 or 47. (William S. Kuba Collection)

FT No. 159 is an example of the freight units rebuilt for passenger service. In this photo a four unit is handling a train into Los Angeles in heavy fog on March 23, 1947. Things are looking good on the Santa Fe even in the heavy fog. (William S. Kuba)

Front view of the No. 50 with its B unit, No. 50A, at the Los Angeles Union Station. (Santa Fe Railway Photo, Harry Stegmaier Collection)

The major component of passenger power from Alco-GE came in the form of the PA-1s and the PA-2s. Both groups consisted of both A and B unit. This photo illustrates the right side of the 51's paint application. (Bob's Photos)

Top down view Alco-GE PA1 No. 51 illustrating the placement of fans and steam generator exhaust systems on both the A and B units.

Part of the Santa Fe newest passenger power came in the form of FP45s from Electro-Motive in 1967, Number series 100 to 108. The units were heavy duty engines with 3,600 horsepower. The 105 and its running mate are between runs at Chicago in this October, 1968 photo. (Harold K. Vollrath Collection)

Still another set of new passenger power came in 1966 from General Electric in the form of U28CGs, originally numbered 350 to 359. The 2800 horsepower units were eventually renumbered 7900 to 7909. The 351 is leading the *El Capitan*, 2nd No. 18 into the Dearborn Station in Chicago on September 22, 1968. (William S. Kuba)

The Santa Fe invested in one set of three units from Fairbanks-Morse, type ALT 100.3. The No. 90 is between runs at Redondo Junction, Los Angeles. (Santa Fe Railway Photo, Harry Stegmaier Collection)

The Santa Fe also invested in 6 3000 horsepower U30CGs from General Electric in 1967, number series 400 to 405. The units were later renumbered 8000 to 8005. These were the last new pieces of passenger motive power to join the Santa Fe before Amtrak. They were painted in the attractive red and silver scheme. The 405 is shown here MU'd with U28CG No. 353 between runs at Kansas City in November, 1969. (Harold K. Vollrath Collection)

The Santa Fe invested in a fleet of road-switchers with steam generators for passenger trains as well as for switching service. GP7 No. 2881 is one example with a steam generator and dynamic brakes. Photographed in service at Lubbock, Texas in November, 1960. (Harold K. Vollrath Collection)

The Santa Fe purchased 8 Alco road-switchers with steam generators. The largest group (five) were the RSD-5s, such as the 2152 shown here at Amarillo, Texas in July, 1961. (Harold K. Vollrath Collection)

The 2882 was repainted in the blue and yellow scheme. This July, 1961 photo was taken at Lubbock, Texas. It is one more color variation in passenger service in addition to the most artistic red and silver. (Harold K. Vollrath Collection)

Chapter 11 - AMTRAK, METROLINK AND COASTER TRAIN SERVICES ON THE SANTE FE

Rolling into the 21st Century, one can still ride passenger trains over the original Santa Fe trackage on Amtrak, or on the new commuter train services out of Los Angeles and San Diego. This is quite to the contrary to what this writer often heard during the 1960s and into the 1970s that not only would the passenger trains have all been discontinued, but literally the entire railroad system would be torn up. If I mentioned anything about coal traffic, or the potential for the railroads to alleviate highway congestion, the answer was usually something like this, "Oh for gosh sakes, wake up and join the progress of the world. Railroads are past history. All we have to do is build more expressways and parking ramps and we can solve America's transportation problems." Well not quite so! Although we have but one transcontinental Amtrak train on the former AT&SF trackage, there are more train services in California with the Amtrak *Surfliners* and the new commuter rail systems than ever before in history. California has now become a model about what can be done for transportation in North America.

AMTRAK

The Santa Fe was pulled into the Amtrak System in May, 1971 along with most of the other railroads offering passenger train services. In fact, only a handful of lines did not originally participate, such as the Southern and the Rio Grande. Eventually, these railroads and their respective routes became part of the Nationwide Amtrak System.

This brief chapter takes a snap shot look at the Amtrak trains on the Santa Fe, primarily in 1971 and then leaping forward three decades. It is indeed fortunate that one can still ride regular passenger trains on the Santa Fe trackage - this does not include, of course, the trackage of the Burlington Northern which is now part of the mega merger known as the Burlington Northern & Santa Fe.

The original name for the Chicago - Los Angeles train service over the Santa Fe was the *Super Chief - El Capitan*, which operated as train 17 and 18. The train provided coach and sleeping car service along with dining and lounge cars. In July, 1971, train 17 departed Chicago at 6:30 p.m. and arrived in LA, two mornings later, at 9:05 a.m. - 40 hours, 35 minute run. Eastbound 18 departed LA at 7:15 p.m. and arrived at the Chicago Union Station at 1:20 the second afternoon, for a 40 hour, 5 minute eastbound run.

Train services on the LA - San Diego included but two daily trains in each direction with the Seattle - San Diego thru passenger train operating to San Diego on Tuesdays, Fridays and Sundays; and from San Diego on Sunday, Wednesday and Friday. It was truly the low end of the passenger train traffic on the San Diego line.

The third Amtrak service consisted of the *Texas Chief*, which operated over the Santa Fe from Chicago to Houston via Fort Worth. Number 15 and 16, the train provided sleeping and coach services as well as a dining car and a dome lounge according to the May 1, 1971 Amtrak timetable.

Things began to change a bit by the April 28, 1973 Timetable. The trains still carried the original names of the *Super Chief*, *Texas Chief* and the *San Diegans*. Service was improved a bit on the line to San Diego with three trains daily in both directions. The Coast Starlight was basically a Seattle - Los Angeles operation with a direct connection with a *San Diegan* in both directions at LA.

Ultimately, the name "Chief" was dropped from the routes over the Santa Fe. The *Texas Chief* became the *Lone Star* and the *Super Chief* was renamed the *Southwest Limited*. What is interesting is that by the mid-1970s, the San Diegans were operated four times in each direction on a daily basis. The San Diegans were equipped with Amfleet equipment according to the October 31, 1976 timetable.

An entire book could be written on the details of the schedules and equipment operated on the Amtrak trains over the Santa Fe trackage. However, the primary focus of this book is on the Santa Fe train services - we have to stay on track. Therefore, leaping ahead to the year 2004, we have some rather incredible operations to report.

The *San Diegans* are now known as the *Pacific Surfliners*. There are 11 trains in each direction Monday thru Thursday. 12 trains in each direction on Friday, Saturday and Sunday.

Another area of increased passenger train services is the Route of the *San Joaquins*. Trains operate over the Santa Fe between Antioch - Stockton - and Bakersfield. There are six trains a day each way to and from Bakersfield. Four are Oakland - Bakersfield trains, while two operate to and from Sacramento. This was once part of the route of the *San Francisco Chief*.

The *Texas Chief* has been long discontinued, but service between Chicago and Texas remains with a train known as the *Texas Eagle*, which operates primarily over the former GM&O and Missouri Pacific routes between Chicago and Fort Worth. South of Fort Worth, the *Texas Eagle* operates over the Santa Fe trackage between Fort Worth and Temple, Texas.

The transcontinental Chicago - Los Angeles train is now known as the *Southwest Chief*. It is equipped with Superliner cars, which in some ways remind one of the Santa Fe Hi-level equipment. In fact, Hi-level equipment actually was part of the Superliner consist and operated as a step-down car between the coaches and the baggage cars. Finally, the *Southwest Chief* now actually operates over the former Burlington Route between Chicago and Kansas City, and thus "Santa Fe" trackage is freight only between the Windy City and KC.

One of the newest Amtrak trains on Santa Fe trackage is the *Heartland Flyer,* an Oklahoma State financed train operating from Oklahoma City to Fort Worth in the morning, and returning in the evening. Trains 821 and 822 provide coach service with meal service. The running time is four hours, 30 minutes for the 206 mile run.

Finally, one can say that California is now the bright star regarding new and expanded passenger services. With the expansion of the *San Diegans* as *Pacific Surfliners*, the new *San Joaquins*, and the addition of the commuter train services (See the next section of this re MetroLink and the Coaster), the former Santa Fe trackage now has more passenger trains than ever in California.. There are few lines in North America that can boast that incredible accomplishment. It shows just what can be done to solve transportation and pollution problems, not to mention substantial improvements in safety for the highway travelers.

METROLINK AND THE COASTER

The Santa Fe operated a wide variety of passenger trains throughout its history including transcontinental streamliners, locals, mail train and many secondary and overnight train operations. The Santa Fe was on the top of the line in terms of services offered to the traveling public. However, one type of service that the company did not operate were the commuter trains. And now since the 1990s, commuter trains are operating on the former AT&SF trackage in the Los Angeles and San Diego areas.

North America is experiencing giant problems with traffic congestion and pollution as well as safety hazards with our highway systems. Passenger trains are the only solution, and California has come to understand how the railroad can provide badly needed services, reduce congestion and pollution, improve safety, and believe it or not, actually improve the economy of both the core cities and suburbs. This is especially important because the cities and suburbs are totally interdependent. An entire book could be written on this concept alone. However, it is time to get back on the Santa Fe tracks and see what is happening in California.

Southern California, as well as the rest of the state, is a bright star for the passenger service concept. Two new commuter rail systems have been established during the early to mid-1990s on three parts of Santa Fe trackage in the Los Angeles and San Diego areas.

Metrolink is the new commuter service in Los Angeles operating over sections of the Santa Fe between LA and Riverside via Fullerton, and also between LA and Oceanside plus a belt line commuter service between San Bernardino and San Juan Capistrano. The belt line cuts off at Orange on the San Diego line and heads north and connects with the main line east of Fullerton.

The other segment of commuter service on parts of Santa Fe trackage is the Coaster line between San Diego and Oceanside, a distance of 41.1 miles. As of 2003, the Coaster is operating 11 trains each way Monday thru Thursday. The frequency increases to 13 trains in each direction on Friday with two evening trains in each direction. There is limited week-end service.

San Diego sees a grand total of 44 passenger trains every weekday, meaning 22 in each direction with the Amtrak and Coaster train services. Much of the San Diego line is now owned by a new railroad company, the San Diego Northern.

Although the commuter trains do not carry the Santa Fe name, one can still enjoy train travel on the Santa Fe routes.

Amtrak began on May 1, 1971. At that time both the *Super Chief* and the *Texas Chief* operated over the Santa Fe from the Chicago Union Depot. At first, the trains were handled by Santa Fe motive power as well as Santa Fe equipment. The trains still carried the Santa Fe numbers 17 and 18 and were listed in the Amtrak time table as the *Super Chief-El Capitan*. This photo by Joe Stark shows No. 17 departing Chicago in October, 1971.

The Santa Fe continued to play a major role in passenger switching. In this case GP20 No. 3168 is shoving the consist for train 17 to the Union Station. Note the former Pennsylvania Railroad coach yards to the right of the photo. (Joseph Stark)

Some of the Santa Fe Hi-level Chair Cars were repainted and re-lettered for Amtrak, such as the 39947. (Bill Jelinek)

The *Texas Chief*, train Numbers 15 and 16, were also assigned Santa Fe equipment with the advent of Amtrak. The *Texas Chief*, shown here at the Chicago Union Station was equipped with a Big Dome Lounge, Hi-level Chair Cars as well as Sleeping cars for the run between Chicago and Houston. (Patrick C. Dorin Collection)

Unless you look very carefully, you're not likely to notice the Santa Fe GP20 at the end of the inbound *Texas Chief*, train 16, pulling the train, units and all out of the Union Station and back to the AT&SF coach yard. By the time this photo was taken in November, 1971, the train had acquired almost a daily dome coach from the former *California Zephyr* - and no longer had the Big Dome Lounge. (John H. Kuehl)

The name *Coaster* decorates the commuter train motive power and equipment operating between San Diego and Oceanside. This Coaster commuter run is rolling through Old Town, just north of San Diego on the former Santa Fe route to Los Angeles. (December 20, 1997, Clifford Prather)

A three car *Coaster* run is rolling along at top speed near Ponto, California on former Santa Fe trackage which is now part of the San Diego Northern. (August, 1997, Clifford Prather)

In May 1972, Amtrak increased the train frequency between LA and San Diego to three trains each way daily. The *San Diegans* were equipped with a variety of Santa Fe and other railroad equipment including Hi-level Chair Cars on train 778 at Fullerton en route from LA to San Diego. (Clifford Prather)

Chapter 12 - BNSF PASSENGER EQUIPMENT AND TRAINS

Amtrak has been in operation since 1971, and the AT&SF and BN merged in 1997. We do not have bright silver passenger trains with the incredible red and silver color scheme for motive power, but we still have passenger equipment with the Santa Fe name in 2004, i.e., Burlington Northern & Santa Fe. In many ways similar to the wide variety of Santa Fe railroads, such as AT&SF, the Gulf Coast and Santa Fe, and the Panhandle and Santa Fe.

Moving into 2004, the company owns a superb fleet of passenger equipment operated for special passenger trains. The special trains include not only business car trains, but also special trips with steam power, company picnics, and many, many other functions. Just one example of the steam powered trains is the Milwaukee Road 261, which has powered trains throughout the mid-west and beyond.

This chapter reviews the current passenger equipment and the business cars with the Santa Fe heritage. The follow rosters and photos tell the story. It is one more way passengers can still ride the Santa Fe all the way.

Business Car Fleet

Car Name	Number
Mississippi River	BNSF01
Columbia River	BNSF02
Red River	BNSF03
Missouri River	BNSF04
Atchison	BNSF05
Topeka	BNSF06
Santa Fe	BNSF07
John S. Reed	BNSF08

Support Equipment

Type	Car Name	Number
Dining Cars	Lake Superior	BNSF10
	Fred Harvey	BNSF11
	Mountain View	BNSF28
	Valley View	BNSF29
Full Dome/ Theater	Glacier View	BNSF30
	Bay View	BNSF31
Track Inspection/ Lounge	William B. Strong	BNSF32
Bi-level Coach	Fox River	BNSF40
	Flathead River	BNSF41

Type	Car Name	Number
	Skagit River	BNSF42
	Rio Grande River	BNSF43
	Colorado River	BNSF44
	Powder River	BNSF45
Sleeper/Power Car	Stampede Pass	BNSF50
Baggage/Power Car	Snoqualmie Pass	BNSF51
Sleeper/Lounge	Deschutes River	BNSF60
Sleeping Cars	Marias Pass	BNSF64
	Raton Pass	BNSF65
	Cajon Pass	BNSF66
	Trinchera Pass	BNSF67
	Rollins Pass	BNSF68
Baggage Car		BNSF77

Railway Service Equipment

Type	Car Name	Number
Track Geometry Car		BNSF80
		BNSF 85
Geometry Support Car		BNSF81
		BNSF86
Research / Test Car	Kootenai River	BNSF82
		BNSF83
Service Car	Rio Grande River	BNSF84
Technical Training Car		BNSF87
		BNSF88
		BNSF99

During the summer of 1998, BNSF operated a special steam-powered train to Superior, Wisconsin, as an employee special. The train was powered by Ex-Milwaukee Road 4-8-4 No. 261. The Power Car "Snoqualmie Pass" was part of the consist to provide power for the air-conditioning and other needs of the passenger consist. The Power Car was coupled behind the Milwaukee Road painted equipment for the 261. (Patrick C. Dorin)

Part of the consist included Baggage Car BNSF 77 painted in the silver colors. (Patrick C. Dorin)

The Santa Fe retained at least two Big Dome Lounge cars after Amtrak for special train services. Two of the cars were part of the 1998 Special and now carry the full Burlington Northern Santa Fe lettering. (Patrick C. Dorin)

Part of the consist included coaches which had been rebuilt from gallery commuter coaches. BNSF No. 44 carries the name Colorado River in the center with the railroad name in full to the right, and the BNSF insignia to the left. (Patrick C. Dorin)

BNSF Coach No. 43, the Rio Grande River shows the lettering with the railroad name to the left, insignia to the right and the car name in the center. (Patrick C. Dorin)

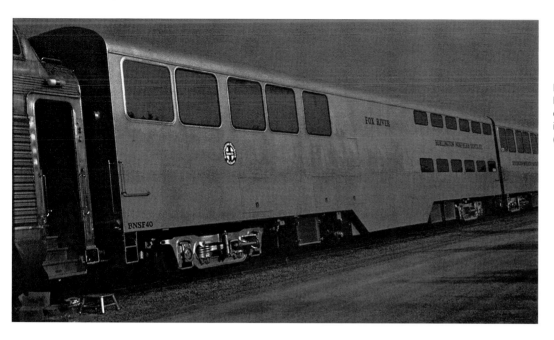

BNSF No. 40, the Fox River, is a lounge car and retains some of the original window arrangements from its commuter rail career days. (Patrick C. Dorin)

Sleeping Car Marias Pass (Patrick C. Dorin)

Sleeping Car Cajon Pass (Patrick C. Dorin)

Sleeping Car Bollins Pass (Patrick C. Dorin)

A BNSF Dining Car was also part of the 1998 consist. (Patrick C. Dorin)

One of the Big Domes was rebuilt with a rear observation window and theatre type in the Dome to view the railroad line as the train rolled along. (Patrick C. Dorin)

The railroad added No. 9964 for power to the end of the train for the back and forth moves of the train between Superior and Saunders for the Employee Special and Picnic. (Patrick C. Dorin)

The original Santa Fe colors of silver and red with the yellow trip lasted into the BNSF merger. In this case, the 8206 has had the initials BNSF applied to the side of the cab. (Patrick C. Dorin)

The 8200 is another example of the Santa Fe colors but in this case, the lettering BNSF graces the side as well as the Santa Fe insignia on the nose. This would be part of the final AT&SF colorscheme into the BNSF merger. (Patrick C. Dorin)

COLOR SECTION

MOTIVE POWER, EQUIPMENT AND MORE

The Santa Fe color scheme for passenger motive power and equipment was most attractive and sent the message. The Santa Fe – All the Way! Alco PA No. 51 displays the color image which was applied to a wide variety of passenger motive power, and even later on freight engines. (Bob's Photo)

Dynamometer cars were assigned the responsibilities of testing out motive power for many operating aspects. The No. 29 is attached to the Alco PA No. 51. (Bob's Photo)

Railway Post Office Cars were an important part of many, if not all, Santa Fe passenger trains for decades until the mid to late 1960s. (Bob's Photo)

The Santa Fe silver color on the passenger equipment stood out in a very attractive and positive way. The Big Dome Lounge Car 507 displays this in a very exciting way. It caught people's attention. (Bob's Photo)

The Gas-electric cars, while painted in the basic Pullman Green colors, carried a red and yellow scheme on the nose. The M-190 is ready to roll at Amarillo, Texas on August 29, 1954. (Joseph Stark)

Car washers are an essential part of passenger train maintenance, and were operated to provide trains en route a quick wash which on their transcontinental runs. (Joseph Stark)

Passenger trains also depended on switch engines for much of the work for assembly, passenger car set outs or pick ups, and for combining or splitting trains at various junction points. Alco S2 No. 2327 is working at Los Angeles on a beautiful May 9, 1954. (Joseph Stark)

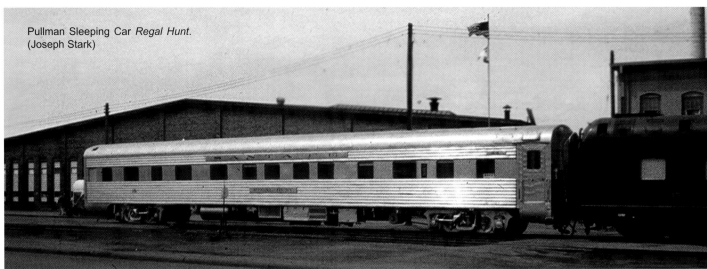

Pullman Sleeping Car *Regal Hunt*. (Joseph Stark)

Business Car *Topeka* (Bill Jelinek)

Heavyweight Business Car No. 37 was repainted in the Silver color scheme which included simulated striping representing corrugated sides. It is shown here at Chicago in June, 1970. (Bob's Photo)

Electro-Motive F unit No. 347C displays the Santa Fe color scheme to its fullest extent in this photo on the head-end of a passenger train at Pasadena, California, which is 9.1 miles east of Los Angeles. (Bob's Photo)

The E-8s, such as the 81, were operated on a number of shorter passenger trains. The 81 is arriving at Pueblo, Colorado and displays the position of the paint scheme arrangements on the E-8s. (Bob's Photo)

The latest passenger power to be purchased and carry the War Bonnet Scheme were the General Electric U30CGs, such as the 404 which shows the paint scheme arrangements on a passenger train at Chanute, Kansas in April, 1968. (Bob's Photo)

TRAINS IN ACTION

Even though it is after the Holiday Travel Season in January, 1964, the *San Francisco Chief*, train No. 1, is at Armarillo is a long train including a container car with mail on the head-end. (Rev. Herman Page)

It is November 1, 1970 and less than a year before Amtrak. Train 78, a *San Diegan*, is pausing ay Santa Ana during its evening run from Los Angeles. (C.R. Prather)

No. 75 is rounding the curve at Fullerton with a three car consist on its run from San Diego to LA in April, 1970. (C.R. Prather)

People are waiting to board as train 74 approaches the Santa Ana depot on November 27, 1970. The Holiday Travel Season is right around the corner. (C.R. Prather)

We have an absolutely glamorous photo of the *Super Chief* powered by 3 Alco PAs rounding a curve displaying the consist of the train shortly after the PAs went into service. (Santa Fe Photo or Bob's Photo, TLC Collection)

The *San Diegans* traveled by and through some incredible scenery between LA and San Diego. In this photo, No. 76 is rolling through a Rock Cut at Miranar in August, 1969. (C.R. Prather)

It is January, 1969 and the Travel Season is still in full swing. Train 75 needs two full units and is powered by No. 404, a U30CG as well as a U28CG at Santa Ana. (C.R. Prather)

Train No. 25 is shown here at Clovis prior to departure for Carlsbad on November 10, 1962. The M-160 is handling one coach for the run in what could be termed a perfect "Pike Size Train" for a variety model railroad layouts. (Rev. Herman Page)

The Santa Fe owned and operated two RDC cars. One of the cars was rebuilt with a baggage compartment. The DC 191 and 192 display the color scheme application after the rebuilding process. (Al Chione)

Train No. 11, the *Kansas Cityan* with the 85 in lead rolls along at Argentine, Kansas in the Summer, 1967 photo. (Rev. Herman Page)

This Dearborn Depot Scene in Chicago shows the westbound *San Francisco Chief* prior to departure with a container car on the head-end in this April, 1963 portrait. (Rev. Herman Page)

The *Tulsan*, Train 211, with two units for power rolls along at Kansas City with its consist of head-end cars and Chair cars with coffee-sandwich cart service between Kansas and Tulsa. The *Tulsan* provided connections with train 19, the *Chief* from Chicago; and train 12, the Chicagoan to Chicago. It is June, 1967. (Rev. Herman Page)

One of many of the unsung heroes of the passenger train business were the switch crews and switch engines which were operated to make up trains, split up trains for a various schedules and the list can go on for a long time. In this photo, we have a switch crew working on train No. 2, the *San Francisco Chief*, while train 25 sits in the background awaiting departure for Carlsbad in February, 1962. (Rev. Herman Page)

Train No. 24, the *Grand Canyon*, is making an important station stop at Albuquerque. The consist includes three head-end cars, one of which is a heavyweight Baggage Car while the other two include a Box Express Car and a REA Express Refrigerator Car. The date is October 7, 1963, and trains 23 and 24 have many years ahead in their career before Amtrak. (Rev. Herman Page)

Train No. 190, the Denver to La Junta local, is pausing at Peublo on a bright summer day in early September, 1967 with a consist of one Chair Car and one Baggage Car. (Rev. Herman Page)

Another view of the Denver-La Junta connecting train in 1969 shows the usual 2-car consist powered by E8m No. 84, one of a very few E units on Santa Fe. (T.W. Dixon, Jr.)

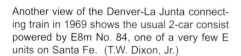

Interior of Santa Fe Chair operating on the La Junta-Colorado connector in June 1969 (T.W. Dixon, Jr.)

The *Texas Chief* is center stage of the superb lighting of the Sun in Chicago on an early Summer day in June, 1969. (Marvin Nielsen)

Equally attractive in many ways are the night scenes of passenger trains. No. 24 has paused for a station stop at Kinsley, Kansas in a late autumn day in November, 1970. (Rev. Herman Page)

There is nothing quite like viewing a train on the Kansas Prairie. The entire consist of the *Chief*, train No. 20 is shown here rolling at top speed on a beautiful spring day in May, 1968. (Rev. Herman Page)

The combine *Super Chief* and the *El Capitan* carried a drum head with both names. We are looking at the rear of train 18 in February, 1967. (Rev. Herman Page)

The last fully scheduled performances of Santa Fe Passenger Services took place in April, 1971. Train No. 23 is departing Chicago with a four car consist. (Robert Bullerman)

This eastbound train, which was photographed at McCook, Illinois, appears to be the *Texas Chief* with a mixed consist of Hi-level Chair Cars, Big Dome Loun Car, Dining Car and Sleeping Cars. It is November, 1970, and traffic levels are lower. In fact, in 1970, there were but four passenger trains in each direction of Chicago. The *San Francisco Chief*, trains 1 and 2; and trains 23 and 24 were on the application block for discontinuance. As a side note: Train 2, the *SF Chi* would have been operating into Chicago during the evening hours – in the dark. (Robert Bullerman)

One never knows when one will see a train at anytime, and anywhere. In this case, a westbound Santa Fe passenger is rolling through Donners Grove, Illinois a detour run over the 3 Track Main Line on the Burlington Northern out of Chicago. It s January 29, 1971, the detour train is kicking up the newly fallen snow w a delightful effect for train watching in the snow. (Robert Bullerman)

The rear end of 24 on that October 7, 1963 day included a Union Pacific 6 Section, 6 Roomette, 4 Double Bedroom sleeping car from the American series. Note the other heavyweight cars in the consist. (Rev. Herman Page)

It is June 25, 1970 and less than a year to the launching of Amtrak. Yet one could still see and ride incredibly beautiful trains All the Way on the Santa Fe. The *San Francisco Chief* is rolling through Joliet, Illinois with the mixed consist of Hi-level Chair Cars, Big Dome Lounge Car and Sleeping Cars, and topped off with a heavyweight Business Car. (Bob's Photo)

To finish off the Color Portfolio, it is time to contemplate the beauty of the Santa Fe passenger services. Here it is early in the morning in November, 1970, and train 24 has stopped at Dodge City before Sunrise and the glow of the red Mars light is poetic and artistic far beyond what words can say about beauty. (Rev. Herman Page)

The U28CG, No. 358 and the U30CG, the 403 headup the *Texas Chief* at Dearborn Station in Chicago in August, 1968. (Al Chione)

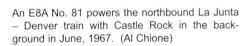

An E8A No. 81 powers the northbound La Junta – Denver train with Castle Rock in the background in June, 1967. (Al Chione)

With an E1 and E2 for power, the Westbound *Kansas Cityan* departs Chicago in June, 1947. (Al Chione)

See the Underground Fairyland
Carlsbad Caverns *Via* Santa Fe

Santa Fe is the only railroad to Carlsbad for Carlsbad Caverns National Park.

Daily Pullman service direct to Carlsbad, New Mexico, from Chicago and Los Angeles

Carlsbad Caverns, in the Guadalupe Mountains of southeastern New Mexico, rank with the Grand Canyon as one of the two or three great natural wonders of the world.

But like trying to describe the Grand Canyon, it is impossible to picture in words the silent grandeur of Carlsbad Caverns—where sunlight has never reached since the dawn of time.

Formations frozen in stone

Fantastic formations frozen in stone, such as Rock of Ages, Chinese Temple, and Lady at the Organ, meet the eye at every turn.

The ceiling has disappeared under millions of stalactite pendants. Grotesque stalagmites, weighing many tons each, rise from the floor.

And the tremendous size of this underground fairyland (temperature, 56° the year 'round) is almost unbelievable.

For instance, the "Big Room" alone is 4,500 feet long, 625 feet wide, 300 feet from floor to ceiling. No photograph yet taken reveals more than an infinitesimal part of its glories.

The way to see it

Plan to visit Carlsbad Caverns via Santa Fe this fall or winter, so you can enjoy an unhurried exploration of *all* parts of the floodlighted Caverns open to the public. U. S. National Park Rangers will be your guides.

Santa Fe provides daily Pullman service from both Chicago and Los Angeles direct to

Carlsbad, New Mexico, where motor coaches meet the train for the 27-mile ride to and from the entrance to the Caverns.

———

Let us send you an illustrated brochure that gives full details on how conveniently you can include this world-famous underground fairyland in your trip to or from California via Santa Fe. Just mail the coupon.

SANTA FE SYSTEM LINES... Serving the West and Southwest
R. T. Anderson, General Passenger Traffic Manager, Chicago 4

Additional examples of Santa Fe's marvelous public relations and advertising programs are shown on the next three pages. They include all three of the AT&SF's PR themes: The Navajo Nation, Southwestern Scenery, and high-end comfort in train accomodations.

Mirage on the Santa Fe

Shades of Francisco Vásquez de Coronado on his search for the Seven Lost Cities of Cíbola—and of Juan de Oñate and his stalwart band on their march across the sun-baked desert! Imagine the travel hardships they bore.

Dreams like these are called up best in the luxury and comfort of a modern streamlined train rolling through a region rich in romance from the past. And nowhere else on rails will you find greater luxury for travel and greater food for dreams than on the famous trains of Santa Fe through our colorful Southwest.

There are soon to be even finer trains on the Santa Fe. Watch for an early announcement.

SANTA FE SYSTEM LINES ... Serving the West and Southwest

History is further used in this nice ad where the ghosts of the Spanish Conquistadors parade along Santa Fe's route. A salute to this heritage is in the train name *El Capitan*.

Santa Fe

..to the colorful Southwest

SANTA FE
ALL THE WAY

That's right, chico.
And "all the way" in the finest modern style—
and now on new and faster schedules.
For Santa Fe feels a great debt to nature for the colorful,
romantic land through which it runs—and
a real responsibility to our patrons, to take them
through it in the finest way.

SANTA FE SYSTEM LINES

Serving the West and Southwest

Santa Fe

Chico, the little Indian boy was often featured on Santa Fe timetables, posters and advertisements. Here a Santa Fe streamliner roars across the historic, scenic, historically romantic vista of the Southwest.